# FRENCH REVIEWED

A REVIEW AND REFERENCE GRAMMAR
FOR COLLEGES

# French Reviewed

## A Review and Reference Grammar
## For Colleges

### IAN FORBES FRASER

*Director, American Library in Paris*

RINEHART & COMPANY, INC.

PUBLISHERS       NEW YORK

Fourteenth Printing March 1957

Copyright 1941, by Ian Forbes Fraser
Printed in the United States of America
*Library of Congress Catalog Card Number: 41-6852*

# PREFACE

*French Reviewed, A Review and Reference Grammar for Colleges,* is the basic unit of a combination of textbooks designed specifically for intermediate instruction in colleges and universities. The trend toward briefer and briefer review grammars has been reversed, since the author's experience leads him to believe that they give unsatisfactory results in training the student to read, write, or speak French. This book presents the major phenomena of the language in greater detail than is customary in such texts; thus it can also be used by all but the most advanced students as a reference grammar throughout college work in French. Instructors who prefer to teach grammar functionally in connection with intensive and extensive reading will find that this text lends itself to such integration.

Accompanying the grammar and based on it is a workbook, the first of a series that will include at least one alternate workbook and a composition and conversation manual. Every teacher has been faced with the annoyance of discarding a satisfactory grammar text, either because the exercises have become stale, or because they have been done by previous owners of secondhand copies. The grammar contains no exercise material, but, by using the workbooks of the series, which may be alternated from year to year, the teacher can give his students extensive and varied drill. Each exercise has been printed on a separate detachable page that may be handed in for correction. This feature should eliminate the possibility that completed exercises will be passed on from one student to another.

Students at the intermediate level in most colleges and universities are drawn from all types of secondary schools, where some have had as much as four years of instruction in French while others have had as little as two, and where emphasis may have been placed on reading, or on grammar, or on the oral use of the language. Consequently, the instructor is under the necessity of bringing students of widely different backgrounds to a common level of attainment, which presumably should be higher than that yet reached by any of them. The present grammar is an attempt to meet this problem by providing explanations that are sufficiently detailed for the weaker students, thus relieving the instructor of the burden of developing each topic in class and freeing the better students from what may frequently become a source of irritation and boredom.

The grammatical material has been divided into fourteen chapters of approximately equal length. Thus, the entire book may be studied in one semester at the rate of one lesson a week. For the convenience of teachers who devote two periods a week to grammar, chapters have been divided into two parts, each of which is a complete unit of work. Supplementary material and reference tables will be found in the appendices. An introduction presents definitions of commonly used grammatical terms for the benefit of the many students who have had no training in formal grammar and to whom the terminology of the subject is frequently as great a mystery as the subject itself.

Each chapter in the grammar is the basis for a set of exercises in the workbook. The first two parts of each set provide relatively easy but thorough drills on the points treated in the corresponding chapter in the grammar, while the third part contains more difficult passages for reading and composition, based on the same points. A verb drill is included in each set of exercises. Since an alternate workbook is now in preparation, suggestions and criticisms will be welcomed from teachers using the first workbook.

Practical teaching devices have been introduced to explain many difficult points in the grammar. Special attention is called to the following: 1) the detailed presentation of the forms and uses of the demonstrative adjectives and pronouns (§16–23); 2) the step-by-step method of handling the combination of demonstrative and relative pronouns (§42); 3) the step-by-step method of building up the reduplicated interrogative pronouns (§50); 4) the careful analysis of the possible translations of *shall* and *will*, *should* and *would* (§62–72); 5) the detailed study of the uses of the past tenses (§74–80); 6) the discussion of the difference between the true and false passives in English, and the analysis of the problem of trans-

# PREFACE

lating them into French (§86); 7) the new approach to the subjunctive, in which stress is put upon understanding principles rather than upon memorizing lists of expressions that do or do not "take" the subjunctive (§91–104); 8) the attempt to systematize the study of the idiomatic uses of **devoir** (§107).

Since it is felt that the study of a foreign language may contribute appreciably to our comprehension of the structure and potentialities of our own language, much emphasis has been laid throughout this book on the similarities and differences between French and English.

In preparing examples for the grammar and exercises for the workbook, vocabulary and idioms have been selected because they were useful in expressing familiar ideas rather than because they appeared at a given level in one or another of the standard word and idiom lists. In the workbook especially, exercises have been based on topics of current or universal interest, with the object of demonstrating to occasionally skeptical American students that it is unnecessary to discuss inanities in speaking a foreign language. The words needed to present such material are in common use in both English and French, although they may be of low frequency in a count based on purely literary selections.

The author wishes to thank all the students and coworkers who have taken an interest in this project and have contributed to it. Especially does he owe his gratitude to his esteemed colleagues and friends, Professor Pierre A. Clamens and Mr. Eugene J. Sheffer, of Columbia University, and Professor Thomas R. Palfrey, of Northwestern University, whose thoughtful suggestions have been deeply appreciated.

I. F. F.

Columbia University
*March, 1941*

# TABLE OF CONTENTS

# FRENCH REVIEWED

A REVIEW AND REFERENCE GRAMMAR
FOR COLLEGES

# INTRODUCTION

## DEFINITION OF GRAMMATICAL TERMS

### I. Sentence.

A sentence is a combination of words that conveys a complete idea. In its simplest normal form it consists of a subject and verb: *He speaks.* Beyond this it may be elaborated to suit the tastes and needs of the speaker or writer. Modifiers may be added to both subject and verb; there may be direct and indirect objects; or, if the verb is some part of *be* (*become, seem, appear, etc.*), there may be predicate nouns, or pronouns, or adjectives. The words that make up a sentence are classified as nouns, pronouns, adjectives, verbs, adverbs, prepositions, conjunctions, and interjections, according to their function in the sentence.

### II. Noun.

A noun is the name of something. A noun may be either the subject of a verb: *The* **man** *speaks;* the object of a verb: *I see the* **man;** the complement of a verb like *be: He is a* **man;** or the object of a preposition: *He is coming with the* **man.**

### III. Pronoun.

A pronoun is a substitute for a noun, eliminating tedious repetition of the noun. Besides the personal pronouns (*I, me, we, us, you, he, him, she, her, they, them, it*), there are other categories of pronouns with special functions:

a) Relative pronouns serve to introduce dependent clauses: *The man* **who** *came to dinner was very interesting.*

b) Interrogative pronouns ask questions: **Who** *is there?*

c) Possessive pronouns (or adjectives) indicate ownership: *This book is* **mine.** *This is* **my** *book.*

d) Demonstrative pronouns point out things to which special attention is called: **This** *is an interesting book.*

*e*) Reflexive pronouns indicate that the doer of an action is also the receiver of that action: *I fooled* **myself.**

*f*) Reciprocal pronouns indicate that two or more persons or things perform an action mutually upon each other: *They saw* **each other.**

*g*) Indefinite pronouns show vagueness about the identity of the persons or things referred to: **All** *can, but* **few** *do.* **Whoever** *can, should go.* **One** *never knows.*

First person pronouns (*I, my, we, us, etc.*) refer to the speaker. Second person pronouns (*you, yours, etc.*) refer to the person spoken to. Third person pronouns (*he, him, her, they, etc.*) refer to the person or thing spoken about.

Since pronouns replace nouns, the noun to be replaced must have been already mentioned, in order to give the pronoun a meaning. The word replaced by the pronoun is called the antecedent of the pronoun. In the sentence: *The man who came to dinner was very interesting,* **man** is the antecedent of **who.** Obviously, no antecedent is needed for pronouns of the first and second persons, for indefinite pronouns, or for interrogative pronouns.

The distinction between conjunctive and disjunctive personal pronouns is made in French but not in English. Roughly speaking, conjunctive pronouns are used in close conjunction with a verb; disjunctive pronouns are not. The exact differences will be discussed in Chapter Five.

## IV. Adjective.

The adjective makes more definite the meaning of a noun or a noun equivalent: *The* **green** *book; I am* **tired.** The adjectives *a, an* are usually called indefinite articles; the adjective *the* is usually called the definite article. Attributive adjectives are used to modify the noun directly and stand right beside it: *The* **green** *book.* Predicate adjectives are used to complete the sense of a verb like *be: I am* **tired.** Adjectives are compared to indicate varying degrees of the quality they describe:

| | | |
|---|---|---|
| Positive Degree | *beautiful* | *bright* |
| Comparative Degree | *more (less) beautiful* | *brighter (less bright)* |
| Superlative Degree | *most (least) beautiful* | *brightest (least bright)* |

## V. Verb.

A verb states something about a noun or pronoun. It expresses an action or a state of being. An active verb is one whose subject performs the action of the verb: *I **hit** him.* A passive verb is one whose subject receives the action of the verb: *He **is hit** by me.* An active verb having a direct object (a noun or pronoun to which the subject does something) is called transitive: *I **hit** him.* An active verb having no direct object is called intransitive: *I **walk**.* Copulative (or linking) verbs are special intransitive verbs that are followed by complements: either nouns, pronouns, or adjectives. Such verbs are: *be, become, seem, appear, feel, taste, smell, look, etc.* Both transitive and intransitive verbs may have indirect objects: *I give **him** the book. I speak **to him**.*

Any verb that agrees with a subject in number and person and so may be used as a predicate is called a finite verb. There are two numbers: singular, and plural; and three persons: first, second, and third, already defined. Finite verbs show time by changes in tense: present (*I go, I am going, I do go*); present perfect (*I have gone*); past (*I went*); pluperfect (*I had gone*); future (*I shall go*); future perfect (*I shall have gone*). Tense names and uses do not correspond exactly in French and English. Differences will be made clear in later chapters. The progressive forms (*I am going, I was going, etc.*) and the emphatic forms (*I do go, I did go, etc.*) do not exist in French, although these same effects are achieved in other ways. Finite verbs are also classified by moods (modes): the indicative, which states a fact or asks a direct question; the imperative, which gives a command; the conditional and subjunctive, whose functions in French differ somewhat from their functions in English, and which will be discussed in detail in later chapters.

The non-finite parts of the verb are: infinitive (*to go*), present participle or gerund (*going*), and past participle (*gone*). Both the infinitive and the present participle may express passive voice or perfect time: *to be seen, being seen, having been seen, to have been seen.*

Auxiliary verbs are used with forms of other verbs to express various shades of meaning. Some auxiliaries indicate change of time: *I have gone, I shall go;* others indicate possibility, ability, or obligation: *I might go, I could go, I should go, I must go. Be* is used to construct the passive: *I am seen; do* is used for emphasis: *I did go.* The translation of these English auxiliaries into French presents many problems, which will be discussed later.

## VI. Adverb.

Adverbs modify verbs: *He speaks **slowly;*** or adjectives: *The snow was **dazzlingly** white;* or other adverbs: *He reads **very** well.*

## VII. Preposition.

A preposition introduces a phrase and always has a noun or pronoun as its object. A prepositional phrase is a word group that does not have a subject and verb. If a phrase modifies a noun, it is adjectival; if it modifies a verb, an adjective, or an adverb, it is adverbial. Adjectival phrases have the same functions as adjectives; adverbial phrases have the same functions as adverbs.

## VIII. Conjunction.

Coordinating conjunctions connect words, phrases, and clauses of equal rank and similar function: *and, or, but, etc.* Conjunctions used in pairs are called correlative conjunctions: *both . . . and, either . . . or, etc.* Subordinating conjunctions introduce dependent clauses and connect them with other parts of the sentence: *although, because, if, since, etc.* Relative pronouns have a similar function, since clauses containing relative pronouns are always dependent.

## IX. Interjection.

The interjection expresses emotion: *Ouch! Alas! Oh!*

## X. Clause.

A clause is a group of words containing a subject and a predicate. The predicate must contain a verb and may contain nothing else: *The man **speaks.*** In the sentence: *The man speaks slowly,* the complete predicate is ***speaks slowly*** (a verb with a modifying adverb). There are two kinds of clauses: 1) independent, and 2) dependent. 1) Independent clauses are complete logical and grammatical expressions. An independent clause is called a simple sentence, if it is punctuated as a sentence: *The man speaks.* 2) Dependent clauses, which begin with subordinating conjunctions or relative pronouns, are incomplete if detached from the sentence of which they form part: *I'll go*, **if I can.** Dependent clauses perform the functions of nouns (noun clauses), adjectives (adjectival clauses), or adverbs (adverbial clauses). Very often words that may be taken for granted are omitted from a clause. This is called ellipsis: *He studied hard while* (**he was**) *in school. He said* (**that**) *he would come.* English uses ellipsis much more frequently than French does. Therefore, it may be necessary to complete mentally an elliptical English clause in order to arrive at the proper basis for a correct translation into French.

## XI. Apposition.

Two or more synonymous expressions not joined by a copulative verb are said to be in apposition: *George VI, King of England.* An appositive is always of the same construction as the word with which it is in apposition, i.e., both words are either subjects, or objects, or objects of a preposition.

## XII. Pleonasm.

A pleonastic word is one whose use seems redundant or superfluous in its clause. Pleonastic words are more common in French than in English.

# CHAPTER ONE

## DEFINITE AND INDEFINITE ARTICLES

### *PART I*

**1. Forms.**

The forms of the definite and indefinite articles in French are:

|  | DEFINITE ARTICLES | INDEFINITE ARTICLES |
|---|---|---|
| Masc. Sing. | **le** | **un** |
| Fem. Sing. | **la** | **une** |
| Masc. or Fem. Sing. before noun beginning with vowel or mute h | **l'** |  |
| Plural | **les** | Partitive **des** (discussed in Chapter Two) |

**2. Use of the Articles.**

In many respects the definite and indefinite articles are used in French as in English. This chapter will discuss the ways in which French usage differs from English.

In French:

*A.* The article agrees in gender and number with its noun.

*Un* homme; *une* femme.  *A man; a woman.*
*Le* livre; *la* musique; *les* amis.  *The book; the music; the friends.*

*B.* The article is repeated before each noun representing a distinctive object. The insistence on parallel structure is carried further: when two or more nouns are governed by the same preposition, especially **à** and **de,** the preposition also must be repeated before each noun. (Remember that à + le = **au;** à + les = **aux;** de + le = **du;** de + les = **des.**)

La population *des* Etats-Unis et *du*  *The population of the United States*
Canada.  *and Canada.*

8

*C.* The definite article appears regularly before nouns used in a general sense. In talking about *all* of an object or about *every* object of a class in English, the article is usually omitted, but this is not so in French. This rule applies to names of abstract things, as some of these examples show:

| | |
|---|---|
| *La* vie aux Etats-Unis. | *Life in the United States.* |
| *L'*amour de *la* patrie. | *Love of country.* |
| *Les* Européens croient que *les* Américains aiment *l'*argent. | *Europeans believe that Americans love money.* |

*D.* Closely connected with this is the use of the definite article before names of languages (which, by the way, are always masculine). Two exceptions should be noted: when the name of the language follows **parler** *directly*, or follows **en,** no article is used.

| | |
|---|---|
| **Nous apprenons** *le* **français.** | *We are learning French.* |
| **Nous parlons** *bien l'***anglais.** | *We speak English well.* |
| BUT: **Les Américains** *parlent anglais.* | *Americans speak English.* |
| **Je sais dire cela** *en* **français.** | *I know how to say that in French.* |

*E.* When a title precedes a proper name, except in direct address, the definite article is necessary. If, in addition, a title of courtesy (**monsieur, madame**) is used, the article must appear.

| | |
|---|---|
| *Le* roi Edouard abdiqua. | *King Edward abdicated.* |
| *Le* docteur Martin est ici. | *Doctor Martin is here.* |
| Je suis bien aise de vous voir, *père* Dupont. | *I am very glad to see you, Father Dupont.* |
| *Monsieur le président* est arrivé. | *The president has arrived.* |
| Entrez, *monsieur le président.* | *Come in, Mr. President.* |

*F.* The definite article frequently stands in place of a possessive adjective. This use is most common with names of parts of the body or of objects closely associated with the person (clothing, etc.). When the replacement of the possessive adjective might lead to doubt as to the ownership of the object in question, clarity is achieved by the use of an indirect object pronoun. For a more complete discussion, see § **37** *C* 1, 2, and 3.

| | |
|---|---|
| **Levez** *la* **main droite.** | *Raise your right hand.* |
| **Il est entré** *le* **chapeau sur** *la* **tête.** | *He came in with his hat on his head.* |

| | |
|---|---|
| Il a mal à *la* tête. | *He has a headache.* |
| Il a *les* épaules carrées. | *He has square shoulders.* |
| Elle *lui* a caressé *les* cheveux. | *She stroked his hair.* |
| Il s'est fait mal *au* pied. | *He hurt his foot.* |

*G.* In indicating price, the definite article replaces the English *a* of: 1) weight, 2) measure, 3) number. When the unit does not fall into one of these categories, **par** is used.

| | |
|---|---|
| Le beurre se vend trente sous *la* livre. | *Butter sells at thirty cents a pound.* |
| Ce drap vaut un dollar *le* mètre. | *This cloth is worth a dollar a meter.* |
| Les œufs coûtent quarante sous *la* douzaine. | *Eggs cost forty cents a dozen.* |
| BUT: **J'ai reçu deux dollars** *par* jour. | *I got two dollars a day.* |

*H.* With the names of days of the week, the use of the definite article indicates the regular recurrence of an event.

| | |
|---|---|
| J'ai ma classe de français *le* lundi, *le* mercredi, et *le* vendredi. | *I have my French class on Mondays, Wednesdays, and Fridays.* |

NOTE: It is equally correct to say **tous les lundis,** etc.

| | |
|---|---|
| BUT: **Il viendra me voir** *samedi* (prochain). | *He will come to see me Saturday (next).* |

*I.* The definite article is used to form the superlative of adjectives (§ 28 *A*).

| | |
|---|---|
| Grand, plus grand, *le* plus grand. | *Big, bigger, biggest.* |

## PART II

### 3. Omission of the Article.

Although French often uses a definite article where English would omit it or would use another word or expression, there are times when French, too, omits the article:

*A.* The article is omitted in many expressions consisting of a verb and a noun. These are usually fixed phrases of idiomatic character. It is unnecessary to give a full list of them, but illustrative examples will be found in reading.

| | |
|---|---|
| *J'ai besoin* d'argent. | *I need money.* |
| Elle *a peur.* | *She is afraid.* |

| | |
|---|---|
| *Faites attention.* | *Pay attention.* |
| Il *a pris congé.* | *He took his leave.* |

*B.* Other fixed phrases, made up of a preposition and a noun and used adjectivally or adverbially, show a similar omission of the article.

| | |
|---|---|
| Il est parti *à pied.* | *He left on foot.* |
| Nous prenons du café *après dîner.* | *We take coffee after dinner.* |
| Il fait chaud *en été.* | *It is warm in summer.* |
| Prenez celui-ci, *par exemple.* | *Take this one, for example.* |

*C.* An unmodified noun, usually one of nationality or profession, standing after the verb **être,** or its equivalent, takes no article. In this case the noun may be thought of as an adjective.   religion

| | |
|---|---|
| Je suis *Américain.* | *I am an American.* |
| Il est *médecin.* | *He is a doctor.* |
| BUT: **Son père est** *un* écrivain distingué. | *His father is a distinguished writer.* |

*D.* The article is omitted before a noun in apposition when that noun serves merely as a parenthetical explanation. This principle explains the omission of the article in numerical titles. However, when the noun in apposition is used to distinguish by contrast or comparison, the article is used as in English.

| | |
|---|---|
| **New-York,** *ville* américaine. | *New York, an American city.* |
| **Henri** *quatre,* *roi* de France. | *Henry the Fourth, king of France.* |
| BUT: **New-York,** *la* plus grande ville américaine. | *New York, the largest American city.* |

## 4. Use of the Article with Names of Countries and Cities.

*A.* The definite article is used with names of countries and continents, especially when these are used as subject or object of a verb.

| | |
|---|---|
| *La* France est un beau pays. | *France is a lovely country.* |
| Beaucoup d'Américains connaissent bien *le* Canada. | *Many Americans know Canada well.* |

*B.* However, certain special rules must be observed:

1) When the name of the country is feminine singular (and this includes the names of all continents and almost all European

countries), *in* or *to* is translated by **en**, and *from* or *of* by **de**, without an article. (See Table, column 1.)

2) When the name of the country is modified (e.g., **l'Amérique du Nord**), *in* or *to* is translated by **dans** + article, and *from* or *of* by **de** + article. (See Table, column 2.)

3) When the name of the country is masculine singular (the important ones are **le Canada, le Mexique, le Japon**), or plural (the important one is **les Etats-Unis**), *in* or *to* is translated by **à** + article, *from* or *of* by **de** + article. (See Table, column 3.)

4) With the names of cities, *in* or *to* is translated by **à**, *from* or *of* by **de**, without an article. An article appears as part of the names of certain cities, of which the most commonly encountered are **la Nouvelle-Orléans** and **le Havre**. (See Table, column 4.)

**C.** These rules have been arranged in tabular form for convenience, and illustrative examples of each case are given below.

|  | FEM. SING. NAMES OF COUNTRIES | NAMES OF COUNTRIES MODIFIED | MASC. SING. OR PLURAL NAMES OF COUNTRIES | NAMES OF CITIES |
|---|---|---|---|---|
| *in, to* | 1) en | 3) dans + article | 5) au (aux) | 7) à |
| *from, of* | 2) de | 4) de + article | 6) du (des) | 8) de |

1) Il est (va) *en* France. — *He is in (is going to) France.*
2) Il vient *de* France. — *He comes from France.*
   Les produits *de* France. — *The products of France.*
3) Il est (va) *dans* l'Amérique du Nord. — *He is in (is going to) North America.*
4) Il vient *de* l'Amérique du Nord. — *He comes from North America.*
   Les villes *de* l'Amérique du Nord. — *The cities of North America.*
5) Il est (va) *au* Canada (*aux* Etats-Unis). — *He is in (is going to) Canada (the United States).*
6) Il vient *du* Canada (*des* Etats-Unis). — *He comes from Canada (the United States).*

| | |
|---|---|
| La population *du* Canada (*des* Etats-Unis). | *The population of Canada (of the United States).* |
| 7) Il est (va) *à* New-York. | *He is in (is going to) New York.* |
| 8) Il vient *de* New-York. | *He comes from New York.* |
| Les gratte-ciel *de* New-York. | *The skyscrapers of New York.* |

# CHAPTER TWO

## THE PARTITIVE. WORDS EXPRESSING QUANTITY. NEGATION

### PART I

**5. Definition of the Partitive.**

The notion of the partitive, fundamental in French, is sometimes difficult for an English-speaking person to grasp. The reason seems to lie in the fact that, while the English noun used in a partitive sense may be preceded by " some " or " any," it very often stands alone. Thus, its form is indistinguishable from that of the same noun used in a general sense. The analysis of the difference in sense in English must be made consciously until the student develops a feeling for the construction.

As the name " partitive " suggests, the construction is used when reference is made 1) to a *part* of the total possible supply of any substance, or 2) to an *unspecified* number of objects of the same class.

1) **Il me donne *de l'*argent.**     *He gives me money.*
2) **J'achète *des* livres.**     *I buy books.*

In these two sentences the English nouns carry no distinguishing sign of the partitive sense, but in French the sign of the partitive, **de,** precedes each noun. This is a rule that must be observed, except in certain cases to be discussed later (§ 8).

The noun used partitively must be distinguished carefully 1) from the noun used in a general sense, and 2) from the noun used in a specific sense:

1) **Les étudiants achètent *des* livres.**     *Students buy books.*

Here we are speaking of students in general; hence the definite article is used. But we are certainly not speaking of books in general, nor of all books, but rather of an undetermined number of them; hence the partitive construction is used.

2) **Je vois *les* roses qui sont sur la table.** *I see the roses that are on the table.*

**Je vois *des* roses sur la table.** *I see roses on the table.*

In the first sentence the noun *roses* refers to a definite group of objects: *all* the roses that are on a specified table; hence the definite article. In the second sentence we are remarking simply that there are *some* roses visible on the table, without specifying the number; hence the partitive construction.

If it is difficult to decide between definite and partitive constructions, the problem may often be reduced to an absurdity by asking the question: Am I referring to *all* of this particular thing that could possibly exist? When an affirmative answer is obviously absurd, the use of the partitive is indicated.

## 6. Forms.

The sign of the partitive, **de,** combines with the definite article: **de + le = du; de + la = de la; de + l' = de l'** (used before a singular masculine or feminine noun beginning with a vowel or a mute h); **de + les = des** (this is the plural of the indefinite article, **un, une**).

## 7. Regular Partitive Construction.

Although English expresses the partitive sense by the noun alone or by the noun preceded by " some " or " any," French regularly puts **de +** the definite article before a noun used partitively.

| | |
|---|---|
| *Des* amis sont venus me voir. | *(Some) friends came to see me.* |
| Elle a acheté *du* pain. | *She bought (some) bread.* |
| A-t-il *de l'*argent? | *Has he (any) money?* |
| Il y a *des* étrangers à New-York. | *There are foreigners in New York.* |

## 8. Omission of Part of the Partitive Construction.

Under certain circumstances the partitive sense is expressed *A*) by **de** alone, without the definite article; *B*) by the noun alone, without either the partitive sign, **de,** or the definite article.

*A.* The partitive is expressed by **de +** the noun:

1) When an adjective precedes the noun or when a noun is understood after an adjective.

**J'ai *de bons* élèves.** *I have good students.*

| | |
|---|---|
| Il a *de ces* idées. | *He has these ideas.* |
| *De grands* arbres et *de petits*. | *Big trees and little (ones).* |

NOTES: *a*) With certain combinations of adjective and noun that are thought of as forming real compounds, the article is not omitted: **des jeunes gens,** *young men;* **du bon sens,** *common sense;* **des petits pois,** *green peas; etc.* *b*) A decree of the French Ministry of Public Instruction permits the use of the article in all cases where the adjective precedes the noun. Most careful speakers and writers do not take advantage of this liberty, although students may come across instances of it in their reading.

2) When a general negation implies that the object or idea represented by the noun does not exist.

| | |
|---|---|
| Il *n'*a *pas d'*argent. | *He has no money.* |
| Elle *n'*a *jamais* eu *de* bonheur. | *She has never had any happiness.* |

NOTE: The construction **ne . . . que** does not imply the non-existence of the object in question. Therefore the definite article is not omitted.

| | |
|---|---|
| Ce magasin *ne* vend *que des* chemises et *des* cravates. | *This store sells only shirts and ties.* |

*B.* The partitive is expressed by the noun alone:

1) After expressions of quantity that govern the noun used partitively by **de** (§ **10** *A*).

| | |
|---|---|
| Donnez-moi *une livre de* sucre. | *Give me a pound of sugar.* |
| Je prendrai *une tranche de* pain. | *I'll take a slice of bread.* |
| J'ai *assez d'*amis mais *peu d'*argent. | *I have enough friends but little money.* |

2) After any expression (frequently verbal) that governs its complement by **de,** and in adjective phrases made up of **de +** noun.

| | |
|---|---|
| J'ai *besoin de* chemises. | *I need shirts.* |
| Il *manque de* courage. | *He lacks courage.* |
| Une bourse *remplie d'*argent. | *A purse full of money.* |
| Le toit est *couvert de* neige. | *The roof is covered with snow.* |
| Une maison *de pierre*. | *A stone house.* |

NOTE: In this construction the meaning changes when a definite article is inserted:

| | |
|---|---|
| Il a besoin *d'*argent. | *He needs money (unspecified amount).* |
| Il a besoin *de l'*argent qu'il vous a prêté. | *He needs the money he lent you (a specific amount).* |

3) After **sans, ni . . . ni,** and, frequently, after **avec**.

| | |
|---|---|
| Je ne peux pas vivre *sans argent*. | *I can't live without money.* |

| | |
|---|---|
| **Il n'a *ni amis ni argent.*** | *He has neither friends nor money.* |
| **Je le ferai *avec plaisir.*** | *I shall do it with pleasure.* |

### 9. *En* as a Substitute for the Partitive Noun.

When a partitive noun is to be replaced by a pronoun, **en** is used to refer to both persons and things. Like other pronoun objects, **en** precedes the verb, except in the imperative affirmative. In any series of pronoun objects, **en** always comes last. There is no agreement of the past participle after **en,** except when an adverb of quantity precedes the verb. As some of the following examples will show, this pronoun is frequently omitted in English. In French, however, it must *never* be omitted. Other uses of **en** will be studied later (§ **34**).

| | |
|---|---|
| **Avez-vous** acheté *des chemises?* — **Oui,** j'**en** ai **acheté. — Combien en** avez-vous *achetées?* | *Did you buy some shirts? — Yes, I did. — How many did you buy?* |
| **Combien** *d'argent* avez-vous? — **Combien en** avez-vous? | *How much money have you? — How much have you?* |
| **J'ai un peu** *d'argent.* — **J'en** ai un peu. | *I have a little money. — I have a little.* |
| **Avez-vous** *des* frères? — **Oui,** j'**en** ai deux. | *Have you any brothers? — Yes, I have two.* |

## PART II

### 10. Words Expressing Quantity.

*A.* Since these common expressions of quantity control following nouns by means of the preposition **de,** the nouns require neither the sign of the partitive, **de,** nor the definite article (§ **8** *B* 1):

| | |
|---|---|
| **assez,** *enough* | **peu,** *little, few* |
| **autant,** *as much (many) as* | **un peu,** *a little* |
| **beaucoup,** *much, many; very much, very many* | **plus,** *more* |
| | **que!,** *how much (many)!* |
| **combien?,** *how much (many)?* | **tant,** *so much (many)* |
| **moins,** *less, fewer* | **trop,** *too much (many)* |

*B.* Two expressions of quantity are followed by **de** + definite article + noun:

> **bien,** *a good deal, a good many, quite a few*
> **la plupart,** *most, the greater part*

17

| | |
|---|---|
| *Bien des* gens le disent. | *A good many people say so.* |
| *La plupart des* livres. | *Most books.* |

*C.* Remarks on the use of words expressing quantity:

1) The preposition **de** is used only when these expressions govern nouns.

| | |
|---|---|
| J'ai *beaucoup d'amis.* | *I have many friends.* |
| BUT: J'ai *beaucoup* travaillé. | *I have worked hard.* |
| Je t'aime *tant.* | *I love you so much.* |

2) Distinguish carefully between **autant,** *as much (many) as,* which implies a comparison, and **tant,** *so much (many),* which does not.

| | |
|---|---|
| Il a *autant* d'argent que vous. | *He has as much money as you.* |
| Nous avons *tant* de blé que nous ne savons qu'en faire. | *We have so much wheat that we don't know what to do with it.* |

3) **Beaucoup** may modify other adverbs, but is never modified except by **pas.** It means both *much* and *very much, many* and *very many;* hence, **très** and **bien** are never used as modifiers of **beaucoup.**

4) **Peu, un peu,** and **quelques** may be confusing:

**Peu** means *few* or *little* with the unhappy connotation of *but few* or *too few.*

| | |
|---|---|
| J'ai *peu* d'amis. | *I have but few friends (unfortunately).* |

**Quelques,** an adjective, on the other hand, is a happier word.

| | |
|---|---|
| J'ai *quelques* amis que j'aime bien. | *(Fortunately) I have a few friends whom I like a great deal.* |

**Un peu,** *a little,* can never mean *a few* and is used only with nouns representing things that are measured, rather than counted.

| | |
|---|---|
| Donnez-moi *un peu* de café. | *Give me a little coffee.* |
| Elle a trouvé *un peu* de tranquillité. | *She found a little peace.* |

5) **Plusieurs,** *several,* is an invariable adjective modifying its noun directly. It does not need the preposition **de.**

| | |
|---|---|
| J'ai vu *plusieurs* livres sur sa table. | *I saw several books on his table.* |

6) *More than* and *less than* before a numeral are translated by **plus de** and **moins de.**

18

**Il a *plus* (*moins*) *de* vingt dollars.**     *He has more (less) than twenty dollars.*

7) When *more* means *an additional quantity of*, use **encore +** du, de la, de l', or des.

**Désirez-vous *encore du* café?**     *Do you wish some more coffee?*

## 11. Negative Expressions.

The negative in French consists regularly of two parts, **ne,** preceding the verb, and some other word or words following it. In the listing below of the principal negative expressions, they have been divided into two groups, for a reason that will appear in § **12.**

*A.* **ne ... pas,** *not*
**ne ... point,** *not* (more emphatic and less common than **ne ... pas**)
**ne ... guère,** *hardly, scarcely*
**ne ... plus,** *no more, no longer*
**ne ... jamais,** *never*
**ne ... rien,** *nothing*

*B.* **ne ... que,** *only, none but*
**ne ... ni ... ni,** *neither ... nor*
**ne ... personne,** *nobody*
**ne ... aucun,** *no, none, not any*

## 12. Position of the Negative.

The following rules govern the position of the negative expression in respect to the verb:

*A.* With simple tenses (**je vois, vous alliez,** etc.), the two parts of the negative are placed before and after the verb.

**Il *ne* parle *pas*.**     *He does not speak.*
**Je *ne* vois *personne*.**     *I see nobody.*

*B.* With compound tenses (**j'ai vu, vous êtes allé,** etc.), the negatives of group *A* in § **11** are placed before and after the auxiliary verb (**avoir** or **être**).

**Il *n'a pas* parlé.**     *He did not speak.*
**Je *n'ai jamais* fait cela.**     *I have never done that.*
**Il *n'a guère* ouvert la bouche.**     *He scarcely opened his mouth.*

19

However, with compound tenses the negatives of group *B* in § 11 are placed before and after the entire verb.

| | |
|---|---|
| Il *n'*a vu *ni* Paris *ni* Londres. | *He saw neither Paris nor London.* |
| Je *n'*ai lu *aucun* de ces livres. | *I have read none of these books.* |
| Il *n'*a connu *personne.* | *He knew no one.* |

*C.* Only conjunctive and reflexive object pronouns (me, te, le, lui, nous, vous, les, leur, se, y, en) can come between ne and the verb.

| | |
|---|---|
| Il ne *me* parle plus. | *He no longer speaks to me.* |
| Je ne *l'*ai pas vu. | *I haven't seen him.* |

*D.* When the negative is used with an infinitive, both parts are placed before the infinitive and its pronoun objects, if any.

| | |
|---|---|
| Il a préféré *ne pas* faire cela. | *He preferred not to do that.* |
| Elle a promis de *ne plus* le voir. | *She promised not to see him again.* |

*E.* The **que** of **ne . . . que** immediately precedes the word it modifies. The word *only* in English should occupy the same relative position, although there is much carelessness in placing this word in the sentence.

| | |
|---|---|
| Je n'en ai acheté *que trois.* | *I bought only three.* |
| Nous n'avons lu *que ce livre.* | *We have read only this book.* |

*F.* To express *neither . . . nor*, **ni** is placed before each co-ordinate word, phrase, or clause. **Ne,** of course, stands before the verb.

| | |
|---|---|
| Qui l'a fait? — *Ni* lui *ni* moi. | *Who did it? — Neither he nor I.* |
| Il *n'*a *ni* amis *ni* argent. | *He has neither friends nor money.* |
| Il *n'*a parlé *ni* à vous *ni* à moi. | *He spoke neither to you nor to me.* |
| Je *ne* veux *ni* que vous lui écriviez *ni* que vous alliez le voir. | *I wish you neither to write to him nor to go to see him.* |

When the co-ordinate elements are the principal verbs of the sentence, **ne** is placed before each of them, while **ni** also must stand before the last of the series.

| | |
|---|---|
| Il *ne* voulait *ni ne* pouvait comprendre. | *He neither would nor could understand.* |

*G.* **Personne, rien,** and **aucun** may be used as subjects and as objects of verbs, and as objects of prepositions. **Ne** must not be omitted, however.

| | |
|---|---|
| *Personne n'*est venu. | *No one came.* |
| Je *n'*ai *rien* vu. | *I saw nothing.* |
| Je *n'*ai parlé à *aucun* de mes amis. | *I spoke to none of my friends.* |

*H.* **Non** plus is used after a negative for emphasis and is usually translated as *either*.

| | |
|---|---|
| Si vous n'en voulez pas, je n'en veux pas *non plus.* | *If you don't want any, I don't either.* |
| Jean ne le voit jamais. — Je ne le vois jamais *non plus.* | *John never sees him. — I never see him either.* |
| Voulez-vous aller les voir ? — **Non.** — Ni moi *non plus.* | *Do you want to go to see them? — No. — Neither do I.* |

## 13. Peculiarities of the Negative.

Many peculiarities in the use of negatives in French will become clear if it is remembered that the second element in most negatives is really a positive word. Thus, **personne** means *a person;* **rien** (from the Latin *rem*) means *a thing;* **jamais** means *ever*. Originally, it was necessary to combine these positive words with the negative **ne** in order to give them negative meaning. Occasionally these words, used without **ne,** still retain their positive sense.

| | |
|---|---|
| **A-t-on** *jamais* vu pareille chose ? | *Has anyone ever seen such a thing?* |
| **Y a-t-il** *rien* de plus beau ? | *Is there anything lovelier?* |

However, these words have been associated with the negative idea for so many centuries that they can be used without **ne** to convey negative meaning, when the verb is omitted.

| | |
|---|---|
| Qui est là ? — *Personne.* | *Who is there? — Nobody.* |
| Etes-vous prêt ? — *Pas* encore. | *Are you ready? — Not yet.* |
| *Plus* de maîtres, *plus* de livres. | *No more teachers, no more books.* |

Remembering the original positive value of these words may help the English-speaking student to understand how the French càn combine two or more negatives around one verb without committing the sin of the " double negative." Such a sentence as: Il *n'*a *jamais rien* dit à *personne,* is correct in French, since **rien** may be interpreted as " anything," and **personne** as " anybody." The negative, then, is single: **ne . . . jamais.**

**14. Use of *Ne* alone.**

**Ne** is used alone with the verbs **oser, pouvoir,** and **savoir,** to soften the negation. The two sentences of the following pairs differ in connotation:

| | |
|---|---|
| { Je *n'*ose le dire. | *I hardly dare say it (but I may).* |
| { Je *n'*ose *pas* le dire. | *I don't dare say it (and I won't).* |
| { Je *ne* peux vous le dire. | *I can't tell you (and I'm sorry).* |
| { Je *ne* peux *pas* vous le dire. | *I can't (and won't) tell you.* |
| { Je *ne* saurais vous le dire. | *I couldn't tell you (but I wish I could).* |
| { Je *ne* sais *pas*. | *I (simply) don't know.* |

**15. Pleonastic *Ne*.**

In certain constructions the French introduce a **ne** that seems superfluous from the English point of view. This is called the pleonastic **ne**. It is used in the second part of unequal comparisons, and in some subjunctive clauses. It will be discussed in connection with those topics (§ 28 *A* 3, § 94).

# CHAPTER THREE

## DEMONSTRATIVE ADJECTIVES AND PRONOUNS

### *PART I*

**16. English and French Demonstratives.**

The demonstrative constructions are more numerous and complex in French than in English. The English words *this, that, these,* and *those* are used as both adjectives and pronouns. Sometimes the words *one* and *ones* are added to the pronoun forms, but that practically exhausts the possibilities of variation. This simple set of English demonstratives is translated into French through the use of several series of forms: 1) the adjectives, always used before nouns and frequently reinforced by -ci and -là; 2) the variable pronouns, used to designate specified persons or objects, when gender and number are known; 3) the invariable pronouns, **ceci** and **cela,** used to distinguish between two unspecified objects whose gender is therefore unknown, or between two ideas; 4) the invariable pronoun **ce,** which may be demonstrative or may simply offer an alternative translation for the third person subject pronouns, *he, she, it, they.*

In general, the demonstratives serve to distinguish between two persons or things, one of which is more remote from the speaker, although this question of distance need not be involved.

**17. Demonstrative Adjectives.**

*A.* The forms of the demonstrative adjective in French are:

MASC. SING. ce (cet)
FEM. SING. cette
}, *this, that*

MASC. PLU. ces
FEM. PLU. ces
}, *these, those*

**Cet** is used before masculine singular nouns that begin with a vowel or a mute h. Notice that **ces** is the plural form for both masculine and feminine; failure to remember this is a common source of error. The demonstrative adjective agrees in gender and number with the noun it modifies.

| | |
|---|---|
| *Ce* livre est intéressant. | *This book is interesting.* |
| *Cet* arbre est un chêne. | *That tree is an oak.* |
| *Cette* jeune fille est très belle. | *That girl is very pretty.* |
| *Ces* jeunes gens sont mes amis. | *These boys are my friends.* |

**B.** In using the demonstrative adjectives, -ci and -là are added to the noun when it is absolutely necessary to distinguish *this* from *that*, or when it is desirable to secure emphasis.

| | |
|---|---|
| *Ce livre-ci* est plus intéressant que ce livre-là. | *This book is more interesting than that book.* |
| *Ces roses-là* sont très belles. | *Those roses are very lovely.* |

**C.** The demonstrative adjective, like the definite article, must be repeated before each noun.

| | |
|---|---|
| *Ces* tableaux et *ces* statues sont des chefs-d'œuvre. | *These pictures and statues are masterpieces.* |

**18. Variable Demonstrative Pronouns.**

**A.** The forms of the variable demonstrative pronoun in French are:

| | | | |
|---|---|---|---|
| MASC. SING. celui | *this (one),* | MASC. PLU. ceux | *these (ones),* |
| FEM. SING. celle | *that (one)* | FEM. PLU. celles | *those (ones)* |

These pronouns agree in gender and number with the nouns that they replace.

**B.** The variable demonstrative pronouns are used to designate specific persons or objects. They obviate the necessity of repeating nouns that have already been used and frequently translate an English possessive noun.

| | |
|---|---|
| *Celui* que nous avons rencontré est mon frère. | *The one (the man) we met is my brother.* |
| J'aime mieux ce film que *celui* que nous avons vu hier soir. | *I prefer this film to the one we saw last night.* |
| Il a vendu son auto et *celle* de son frère. | *He sold his own car and his brother's.* |

**C.** The demonstrative pronoun must be followed either by a relative clause, or by a phrase introduced by de, or by -ci or -là; but -ci or -là is not added when the demonstrative pronoun is accompanied by a relative clause or a de phrase.

| | |
|---|---|
| Nous avons besoin de deux chaises: apportez *celle qui est dans le salon* et *celle-ci* aussi. | *We need two chairs: bring the one that is in the parlor and this one too.* |
| De ces deux livres, je préfère *celui de Dumas* à *celui-là.* | *Of these two books, I prefer the one by Dumas to that one.* |

**D.** The use of **celui-ci** and **celui-là** to contrast *the latter* with *the former* is sometimes confusing. In tracing back along the printed lines on a page, *the latter* would be encountered first. Since it is the nearer, it is designated by **celui-ci,** while *the former*, being farther away, is designated by **celui-là.**

| | |
|---|---|
| J'ai un frère, Jean, et une sœur, Marie; *celle-ci* a dix-huit ans, *celui-là* en a seize. | *I have a brother, John, and a sister, Mary; the latter is eighteen, and the former is sixteen.* |
| Le Canada et le Mexique sont nos voisins; *celui-ci* est au sud, *celui-là* est au nord des Etats-Unis. | *Canada and Mexico are our neighbors; the latter is to the south, the former is to the north of the United States.* |

**19. Invariable Demonstrative Pronouns, *Ceci* and *Cela*.**

**A.** Ceci means *this, the nearer;* **cela** (ça, colloquially) means *that, the more remote.*

**B.** Since **ceci** and **cela** are used to refer to something indicated, but not yet named, they can have no gender. They must not be used instead of **celui-ci** (**-là**) to refer to named or clearly suggested objects, whose gender is therefore known. **Ceci** may also refer to a whole idea about to be mentioned, and **cela** to an idea already mentioned.

| | |
|---|---|
| J'aime *ceci* mais je préfère *cela.* | *I like this but prefer that.* |
| Regardez *ceci.* Qu'est-ce que c'est? | *Look at this. What is it?* |
| Rappelez-vous *ceci:* Je ne veux pas le voir. | *Remember this: I don't want to see him.* |
| A-t-il dit *cela?* | *Did he say that?* |
| *Ça* ne fait rien. | *That doesn't matter.* |

**C.** Ceci and cela may be divided into their component parts before the verb être + a predicate noun.

| | |
|---|---|
| *Ceci* est un fait.} *C'est ici* un fait.} | *This is a fact.* |
| *C'est là* un fait. | *That is a fact.* |

## PART II

### 20. The Pronoun *Ce*.

The invariable demonstrative pronoun **ce** may translate any one of these subject pronouns: *he, she, it, they, this, that, these, those.* It also stands as an antecedent to a relative pronoun, and as such may be either the subject or direct object of a verb or the object of a preposition. Sometimes its use for emphasis in French is pleonastic as compared with English and is, therefore, untranslatable (§ 23).

### 21. *Ce* or *Il* as the Subject of *Etre*.

One of the student's major problems will be to learn when to use **ce** rather than **il** (**elle, ils, elles**) as the subject of the verb **être**. The decision depends on what follows **être**.

*A.* **Ce** translates *he, she, it, they, this, that, these,* or *those* when **être** is followed by:

1) A modified noun (the modifier may be nothing more than an article).

| | |
|---|---|
| *C'est un professeur.* | *He is a professor.* |
| *C'est une belle jeune fille.* | *She (that) is a lovely girl.* |
| *Ce sont de vieux amis.* | *They (these, those) are old friends.* |
| *C'est une histoire intéressante.* | *It (this, that) is an interesting story.* |

2) A pronoun.

| | |
|---|---|
| *C'est moi (toi, lui, elle, nous, vous).* | *It is I (you, he, she, we, you).* |
| *Ce sont eux (elles).* | *It is they. (They are the ones.)* |
| *C'est cela.* | *That's it.* |
| *C'est celui qui nous a parlé.* | *He is the one who spoke to us.* |

3) A proper name.

| | |
|---|---|
| *C'est Jean (Marie).* | *It (this, that) is John (Mary).* |

4) A superlative.

| | |
|---|---|
| *C'est le meilleur.* | *It is the best.* |
| *C'est le plus grand de tous.* | *It (this) is the largest of all.* |

*B.* **Ce** translates *it, this,* or *that* when **être** is followed by:

1) An adjective that does not refer to a specific noun.

| | |
|---|---|
| Le sujet est assez difficile. — C'est *vrai*. | *The subject is fairly difficult. — That is true.* |
| Venez tout de suite, *c*'est très *important*. | *Come at once, it is very important.* |

2) An adverb.

| | |
|---|---|
| C'est *beaucoup trop*. | *It (this, that) is far too much.* |
| *Combien* est-ce? | *How much is it (this, that)?* |

3) An infinitive.

| | |
|---|---|
| C'est tout *dire*. | *That is telling everything.* |
| *Ce* serait *perdre* tous mes amis. | *That would be losing all my friends.* |

4) A prepositional phrase or a conjunction.

| | |
|---|---|
| C'est *pour vous*. | *It (this, that) is for you.* |
| C'est *pourquoi* je l'ai dit. | *That is why I said it.* |

**C.** Il (elle, ils, elles) translates *he, she, it,* or *they* when être is followed by:

1) An unmodified noun (usually a noun of profession or nationality).

| | |
|---|---|
| *Il* est *professeur*. | *He is a professor.* |

    COMPARE: *C*'est *un professeur*.    *He is a professor.*

| | |
|---|---|
| *Elle* est *Française*. | *She is French.* |
| *Ils* sont *amis*. | *They are friends.* |

2) An adjective referring to a specific person or thing.

| | |
|---|---|
| *Il* est très *vieux*. | *He is very old.* |
| *Elle* est presque trop *intelligente*. | *She is almost too bright.* |
| Avez-vous lu ce livre? — Oui, *il* est bien *écrit*. | *Have you read this book? — Yes, it is well written.* |
| J'ai vu une pièce de théâtre hier soir. *Elle* était peu *intéressante*. | *I saw a play last night. It was rather dull.* |

3) An hour of the day.

| | |
|---|---|
| *Il* est *minuit* (*quatre heures*). | *It is midnight (four o'clock).* |

**D.** A special problem is presented when an infinitive is dependent upon an adjective that follows être. In English the two sentences, *It is easy to do that,* and *That is easy to do,* are equivalent in meaning. In the first, however, the pronoun *it* merely anticipates the real subject, "to do that," which is to be mentioned later in the sentence. In the second, no further explanation of the pronoun *that* is given in the sentence. These sentences are translated into French as follows:

*Il* est facile *de* faire cela.       *It is easy to do that.*
*C'est* facile *à* faire.       *That is easy to do.*

Thus, when the pronoun *it* is to be explained later in the same sentence, *it* is translated by **il,** and the connective between adjective and infinitive is the preposition **de.** When, however, the initial pronoun is not explained later in the same sentence, that pronoun is translated by **ce,** and the connective between adjective and infinitive is the preposition **à.** Other examples:

*Il* est urgent *de* partir tout de suite.       *It is urgent to leave at once.*
*Il* est impossible *de* vous comprendre.       *It is impossible to understand you.*
*C'est* impossible *à* comprendre.       *That is impossible to understand.*

The pronoun *it* may be explained by a **que** clause, as well as by **de** + an infinitive. Naturally, it is then translated by **il.**

*Il* est clair *que vous mentez.*       *It is clear that you are lying.*
*Il* est possible *qu'il soit ici.*       *It is possible that he is here.*

**22.** *Ce* **as Antecedent to a Relative Pronoun.**

The combination **ce** + a relative pronoun translates *that which, what, which, etc.* The handling of the relative pronoun part of this construction will be discussed in Chapter Six. For the moment, it is important to remember that **ce** is not part of the relative clause and that it does its job in its own clause independently of the function and construction of the relative pronoun. The antecedent **ce** may be:

*A.* A subject.

*Ce* | qu'il m'a dit | est vrai.       *What (that which) he told me is true.*

*B.* A direct object of a verb.

Je crois *ce* | qu'il m'a dit |.       *I believe what he told me.*

*C.* An object of a preposition.

Je pense souvent à *ce* | qu'il disait |.       *I often think of what he used to say.*

*D.* A summarizing word, standing for a whole idea, which would be too vague an antecedent for the relative pronoun.

Il est très intelligent, *ce* | qui me    *He is very intelligent, which pleases*
plaît |.                          *me.*

> NOTE: **Ce** represents the whole idea, **Il est très intelligent.**

### 23. *Ce* as Used for Emphasis.

The pronoun **ce** is useful in many combinations to bring into sharper relief one element of a sentence. In some of the following examples, **ce,** used in this way, is pleonastic as compared with English usage and is, therefore, untranslatable. Some possible constructions:

**C'est moi qui le dis.**           *It is I who say so.*
INSTEAD OF: **Je le dis.**

**Celui qui l'a fait c'est vous.**      *The one who did it is you.*
INSTEAD OF: **Vous l'avez fait.**

**Ce qu'il veut c'est de l'argent.**    *What he wants is money.*
**C'est de l'argent qu'il veut.**
INSTEAD OF: **Il veut de l'argent.**

**C'est une bonne idée que la vôtre.**   *That's a good idea of yours.*
INSTEAD OF: **Votre idée est bonne.**

# CHAPTER FOUR

## NOUNS AND ADJECTIVES

### *PART I*

**24. Gender of Nouns.**

French nouns are either masculine or feminine. In studying vocabulary, the student should learn the gender of a noun as well as its correct spelling. Many plans have been devised to simplify the problem of remembering genders, but they are unsatisfactory because of the numerous exceptions to the rules. It is best, therefore, to accept the fact that there is no real short cut to the learning of French genders. Nevertheless, a few suggestions, tentatively offered, may be of some slight help.

Most French nouns are derived from Latin nouns, and it is natural that Latin masculines should appear as masculines in French, Latin feminines as feminines in French. This rule is not absolute, however, and the situation is further complicated by the many neuter nouns in Latin that had to become either masculine or feminine in French. All that can be said is that the student knowing Latin genders has a better than even chance of determining French genders correctly through the use of that knowledge. Then, too, nouns of similar ending tend to be of the same gender. Thus, most nouns that end in a vowel other than **mute e** or that end in a consonant are masculine, while most of those ending in a **mute e** preceded by a vowel or a double consonant are feminine. Other hints of this kind could be given, but here again there are long lists of exceptions. It might be assumed that names of male beings would always be masculine, those of female beings always feminine, but even this is not true. For example, most nouns denoting profession have no feminine form, and it is necessary to say: **Willa Cather est *un* auteur distingué.** Other nouns are always feminine, whether referring to males or females: **la personne, la dupe, la victime,** and, curiously enough, **la sentinelle,** *sentry,* and **la recrue,** *recruit.* To confuse matters, some nouns are of double gender. In such words as **un** or **une artiste, un** or **une enfant, un** or **une élève,** etc., the meaning does not vary with the gender. But the following, among others, change their meaning:

| | |
|---|---|
| le critique, *critic* | la critique, *criticism* |
| le livre, *book* | la livre, *pound* |
| le page, *page-boy* | la page, *page of a book* |
| le tour, *turn, trick* | la tour, *tower* |
| le voile, *veil* | la voile, *sail* |

It should be apparent that tricky devices to simplify the learning of gender are relatively useless. The best solution seems to be the first suggested: Each noun should be memorized with its appropriate article. The student will make mistakes occasionally, but so do native-born Frenchmen.

## 25. Formation of the Feminine of Adjectives and Nouns.

The formation of the feminine is so often parallel in nouns and adjectives that it is convenient to consider this as one subject of study.

*A.* To form the feminine of an adjective or noun, –e is regularly added to the masculine singular. If this form already ends in –e, no change is made.

| Adjectives | | Nouns | |
|---|---|---|---|
| MASC. | FEM. | MASC. | FEM. |
| grand, *tall* | grande | cousin, *cousin* | cousine |
| vert, *green* | verte | voisin, *neighbor* | voisine |
| joli, *pretty* | jolie | ami, *friend* | amie |
| têtu, *stubborn* | têtue | Louis, *Louis* | Louise |
| jeune, *young* | jeune | artiste, *artist* | artiste |
| rouge, *red* | rouge | élève, *pupil* | élève |

A few nouns add –esse to the final consonant of the masculine singular. This sometimes involves a change in the stem. These are very common ones:

| MASC. | FEM. | MASC. | FEM. |
|---|---|---|---|
| comte, *count* | comtesse | dieu, *god* | déesse |
| hôte, *host* | hôtesse | duc, *duke* | duchesse |
| maître, *master* | maîtresse | nègre, *negro* | négresse |
| prince, *prince* | princesse | | |

*B.* Irregular feminines of adjectives and nouns follow these rules:

1) Some final consonants are changed before –e is added.

–c becomes –ch–:
| | |
|---|---|
| blanc, *white* | blanche |
| franc, *frank* | franche |
| sec, *dry* | sèche |

EXCEPTION: public, *public*    publique

–eur becomes –euse:
| | |
|---|---|
| flatteur, *flattering, flatterer* | flatteuse |
| rêveur, *dreamy, dreamer* | rêveuse |
| menteur, *lying, liar* | menteuse |
| danseur, *dancer* | danseuse |
| chanteur, *singer* | chanteuse |

EXCEPTIONS: meilleur, and those in –érieur are regular.

–f becomes –v–:
| | |
|---|---|
| actif, *active* | active |
| bref, *short* | brève |
| neuf, *new* | neuve |
| veuf, *widower* | veuve |

–g becomes –gu–:   long, *long*       longue

–x becomes –s–:
| | |
|---|---|
| heureux, *happy* | heureuse |
| jaloux, *jealous* | jalouse |
| nombreux, *numerous* | nombreuse |
| époux, *husband* | épouse |

EXCEPTIONS:
| | |
|---|---|
| doux, *sweet* | douce |
| faux, *false* | fausse |

2) Adjectives and nouns ending in –el, –eil, –ien, –on, and frequently –s and –t, double the final consonant before –e.

| MASC. | FEM. | MASC. | FEM. |
|---|---|---|---|
| cruel, *cruel* | cruelle | lion, *lion* | lionne |
| pareil, *similar* | pareille | gros, *large* | grosse |
| ancien, *old* | ancienne | bas, *low* | basse |
| canadien, *Canadian* | canadienne | sot, *stupid* | sotte |
| chien, *dog* | chienne | chat, *cat* | chatte |
| bon, *good* | bonne | | |

ADD:

| MASC. | FEM. | MASC. | FEM. |
|---|---|---|---|
| paysan, *peasant* | paysanne | gentil, *nice* | gentille |

EXCEPTIONS:
| | |
|---|---|
| gris, *gray* | grise |
| idiot, *idiotic* | idiote |
| prêt, *ready* | prête |

3) Five common adjectives have two masculine forms:

| MASC. | FEM. | MASC. | FEM. |
|---|---|---|---|
| beau, bel, *fine* | belle | nouveau, nouvel, *new* | nouvelle |
| fou, fol, *mad* | folle | vieux, vieil, *old* | vieille |
| mou, mol, *soft* | molle | | |

The masculine form ending in –l is used before a word beginning with a vowel or a mute h. The feminine is derived from this form by the principle stated in § 2, above.

4) The ending –er becomes –ère, and in a few words –et becomes –ète.

| MASC. | FEM. | MASC. | FEM. |
|---|---|---|---|
| cher, *dear* | chère | complet, *complete* | complète |
| fier, *proud* | fière | discret, *discreet* | discrète |
| berger, *shepherd* | bergère | inquiet, *uneasy* | inquiète |
| étranger, *stranger* | étrangère | secret, *secret* | secrète |

5) Most adjectives and nouns ending in –teur have feminines in –trice.

| | | | |
|---|---|---|---|
| acteur, *actor* | actrice | directeur, *director* | directrice |

6) Three irregular feminines:

| | | | |
|---|---|---|---|
| frais, *fresh* | fraîche | héros, *hero* | héroïne |
| favori, *favorite* | favorite | | |

7) Some nouns denoting living beings distinguish between the masculine and feminine by the use of different words.

| MASC. | FEM. | MASC. | FEM. |
|---|---|---|---|
| bœuf, *ox* | vache | oncle, *uncle* | tante |
| frère, *brother* | sœur | roi, *king* | reine |
| homme, *man* | femme | vieillard, *old man* | vieille |
| mari, *husband* | femme | | |

## PART II

## 26. Formation of the Plural of Adjectives and Nouns.

*A.* The plural of an adjective or a noun is regularly formed by adding –s to the singular.

Livre(s); sœur(s); grand(s), grande(s)     *Book(s); sister(s); tall*

*B.* Nouns with certain endings offer exceptions to this general rule. Adjectives with corresponding endings usually follow the model of the noun.

1) Nouns and masculine adjectives ending in –s or –x remain unchanged in the plural.

| Sing. | Plu. | Sing. | Plu. |
|---|---|---|---|
| le bras, *arm* | les bras | gris, *gray* | gris |
| la noix, *nut* | les noix | vieux, *old* | vieux |
| Note also: le nez, *nose* | les nez | | |

2) Nouns and masculine adjectives in –au take –x.

château(x), *castle*(s)　　　　　　　　beau(x), *fine*

3) Nouns in –eu take –x; masculine adjectives in –eu take –s.

feu(x), *fire*(s)　　　　　　　　　　bleu(s), *blue*

4) Seven nouns in –ou take –x; all others take –s.

| | |
|---|---|
| bijou(x), *jewel*(s) | hibou(x), *owl*(s) |
| caillou(x), *pebble*(s) | joujou(x), *toy*(s) |
| chou(x), *cabbage*(s) | pou(x), *louse, lice* |
| genou(x), *knee*(s) | But: clou(s), *nail*(s) |

5) Most nouns and masculine adjectives in –al regularly change –al to –au– and add –x.

le cheval, *horse* les chevaux　　　　spécial, *special* spéciaux

The only important noun exception to this rule is le bal, *dance,* whose plural is les bals. The masculine plural of some adjectives in –al has never been determined, and writers usually avoid these forms.

6) A few nouns in –ail have a plural in –aux.

| | | | |
|---|---|---|---|
| le corail, *coral* | les coraux | le vitrail, *stained glass* | les vitraux |
| le travail, *work* | les travaux | *window* | |

7) Three irregular plurals:

| | | | |
|---|---|---|---|
| un aïeul, *ancestor* | des aïeux | un œil, *eye* | des yeux |
| le ciel, *sky* | les cieux | | |

*C.* In compound nouns only the noun and adjective components may take the sign of the plural. Even these may be pluralized only when the plural idea clearly belongs to them. Following are some common compound nouns with their plural forms:

grand'mère(s), *grandmother(s)*

grand(s)-père(s), *grandfather(s)*

monsieur (messieurs), *Mr. (Messrs.)*

madame (mesdames), *Mrs.*

mademoiselle (mesdemoiselles), *Miss(es)*

chef(s)-d'œuvre, *masterpiece(s)*

tête-à-tête, *private interview* (not pluralized, since in *each* private interview only two people can get their heads together)

réveille-matin, *alarm clock* (not pluralized, since the plural idea does not belong to the noun, **matin**)

*D.* Names of persons and families are invariable in the plural.

Les *Dupont* sont ici.    *The Duponts are here.*

When, however, proper names are used as common nouns, the sign of the plural is used.

Les *Shakespeares,* les *Miltons,* les *Molières* sont rares.    *Shakespeares, Miltons, and Molières are rare.*

## 27. Agreement of Adjectives.

*A.* An adjective agrees in number and gender with the noun it modifies.

*Cette* pièce est *intéressante.*    *That play is interesting.*

C'est *une bonne* pièce.    *That is a good play.*

*B.* An adjective modifying two nouns is plural. If the two nouns differ in gender, the adjective is masculine plural.

Des pommes et des pêches *mûres.*    *Ripe apples and peaches.*

Un après-midi et une soirée *chargés.*    *A busy afternoon and evening.*

*C.* Some adjectives are used as adverbs; they are then invariable.

Cette fleur sent *bon.*    *This flower smells sweet.*

La robe lui a coûté *cher.*    *The dress cost her a lot.*

*D.* When the adjective **demi,** *half,* is used to indicate less than one full unit of measurement, it precedes the noun and is connected to it by a hyphen; it is then invariable. In indicating more than one full unit, **demi** follows the noun and agrees with it in gender.

Une *demi*-livre; une livre et *demie.* *Half a pound; a pound and a half.*

## 28. Comparison of Adjectives.

*A.* Adjectives are regularly compared as follows:

| POSITIVE | COMPARATIVE | SUPERLATIVE |
|---|---|---|
| fort, *strong* | plus fort, *stronger* | le plus fort, *strongest* |
| | moins fort, *less strong* | le moins fort, *the least strong* |
| | aussi fort, *as strong* | |

1) **Plus** (**moins, aussi**) and **le plus** (**le moins**) are repeated before each adjective compared. *Than* or *as* is translated by **que.**

Jean est *le plus* intelligent et *le plus* sérieux de tous.
*John is the most intelligent and serious of all.*

Jean est *plus* (*aussi*) grand *que* moi.
*John is taller (as tall) than (as) I.*

2) After a negative, **aussi** is replaced by **si.**

Il n'est pas *si* grand que moi.
*He is not so tall as I.*

NOTE: In conversational French, this rule is frequently not observed.

3) A pleonastic **ne** is usually used in the second clause of an unequal comparison.

Il est plus sérieux qu'il *ne* paraît.
*He is more serious than he seems.*

4) The definite article of the superlative may be replaced by a possessive adjective. Both show the gender and number of the noun modified.

*Mes* plus jeunes amis.
*My youngest friends.*

Cette fleur est *la* plus belle.
*This flower is the most beautiful.*

5) A superlative adjective occupies the position relative to its noun that it would occupy in the positive. When a superlative follows the noun, the definite article must not be omitted.

*La plus jolie* jeune fille.
*The prettiest girl.*

La jeune fille *la plus intelligente.*
*The most intelligent girl.*

6) After a superlative, *in* is translated by **de.**

L'élève le plus intelligent *de* la classe.
*The most intelligent student in the class.*

La plus grande ville *du* Canada.
*The largest city in Canada.*

7) The comparative and superlative are indistinguishable in form in French when the article is required before the comparative.

| | |
|---|---|
| *Le plus cher* de ces deux livres. | *The more expensive of these two books.* |
| *Le plus cher* de mes livres. | *The most expensive of my books.* |

**B.** Three adjectives in French are compared irregularly:

| POSITIVE | COMPARATIVE | SUPERLATIVE |
|---|---|---|
| bon, *good* | meilleur | le meilleur |
| mauvais, *bad* | pire (plus mauvais) | le pire (le plus mauvais) |
| petit, *small* | moindre (plus petit) | le moindre (le plus petit) |

1) **Pire** is stronger than **plus mauvais,** and frequently carries the idea of *more evil, more wicked.*

| | |
|---|---|
| Cette pièce est *plus mauvaise* que l'autre. | *That play is worse than the other.* |
| C'est *le pire* de tous les crimes. | *That is the worst of all crimes.* |

2) **Moindre** usually means *less in importance;* **plus petit,** *less in size.*

| | |
|---|---|
| Cette affaire est de la *moindre* importance. | *This affair is of the least significance.* |
| Ce livre est *plus petit.* | *This book is smaller.* |

## 29. Position of Adjectives.

**A.** No rules for the position of attributive adjectives can be absolute. To convey an exact shade of meaning, an author may decide to alter the established position of an adjective with respect to its noun. In the examples analyzed below, certain general principles may be observed: 1) a following adjective is usually used in its literal sense to describe a specific or distinguishing characteristic of the noun; 2) a preceding adjective is usually used in a figurative sense, or is used to describe a quality essential to the noun:

| | |
|---|---|
| 1) **Une rose** *blanche.* | *A white rose (not all roses are white).* |
| **Un homme** *intelligent.* | *An intelligent man (not all are).* |
| **Le drapeau** *américain.* | *The American flag (other nations have flags).* |
| **Un homme** *maigre.* | *A thin man (not all men are thin).* |
| 2) **Un** *maigre* **repas.** | *A scanty meal (figurative sense).* |
| **Un** *savant* **professeur.** | *A learned professor (the idea of learning is naturally associated with a professor).* |

Une *prodigieuse* aventure.    *An extraordinary adventure (adventures may well be extraordinary).*

Une *noire* pensée.    *A gloomy thought (figurative sense).*

    *B.* Certain very common adjectives generally precede the noun:

| beau<br>joli<br>vilain | bon<br>mauvais | court<br>long | grand<br>gros<br>petit | jeune<br>vieux | sot |

    *C.* Many adjectives vary in meaning as they precede or follow the noun. In general, these variations depend on the principles already stated, but frequently they are too subtle to analyze closely. The student should watch for them in his reading and try to become familiar with the differences in meaning. A few common examples:

| | |
|---|---|
| Un *certain* homme.<br>Une nouvelle *certaine.* | *A certain man.*<br>*An authenticated piece of news.* |
| Un *cher* ami.<br>Une automobile *chère.* | *A dear friend.*<br>*An expensive automobile.* |
| Un *dernier* effort.<br>La semaine *dernière.* | *A last effort (of a series).*<br>*The past week.* |

    *D.* When two or more adjectives accompany a noun, the position of each is determined by its own rule. When they are joined by a conjunction, all must follow the noun, in case one would normally follow.

Un *grand jeune* homme.    *A tall young man.*
Une *belle* perle *noire.*    *A beautiful black pearl.*
Un chevalier *jeune et audacieux.*    *A bold young knight.*

    *E.* The position of the predicate adjective in these French sentences does not conform with English usage:

Que (Comme) je suis *content* de vous voir !    *How glad I am to see you !*
Il est assez *intelligent.*    *He is intelligent enough.*

# CHAPTER FIVE

## PERSONAL PRONOUNS. *Y* AND *EN*. POSSESSIVES

### *PART I*

### 30. Conjunctive and Disjunctive Pronouns.

The functions of these two sets of personal pronouns in French are suggested by their names. Generally speaking, the conjunctive pronoun is intimately joined to the verb as subject or object; the disjunctive, on the other hand, is used apart from the verb. Another distinction may be made: The conjunctives are unstressed forms, while the disjunctives are stressed. Compare the force of the first person singular pronouns in these two sentences: *Je* le dis; **Qui le dit?** — *Moi.* A rather ungrammatical parallel may be found in the tendency of English popular speech to replace " It's I " by the much more assertive " It's me." Whether conjunctive or disjunctive, the personal pronoun agrees with its antecedent in person, number, and gender.

### 31. Forms of the Conjunctive and Disjunctive Pronouns.

*Singular*

| PERSON | SUBJ. | DIR. OBJ. | IND. OBJ. | DISJUNCTIVE |
|---|---|---|---|---|
| 1st | je | me | me | moi |
| 2nd | tu | te | te | toi |
| 3rd Masc. | il | le | lui | lui |
| 3rd Fem. | elle | la | lui | elle |

*Plural*

| PERSON | SUBJ. | DIR. OBJ. | IND. OBJ. | DISJUNCTIVE |
|---|---|---|---|---|
| 1st | nous | nous | nous | nous |
| 2nd | vous | vous | vous | vous |
| 3rd Masc. | ils | les | leur | eux |
| 3rd Fem. | elles | les | leur | elles |

## 32. The Reflexive and Reciprocal Pronouns.

*A.* The forms of the reflexive and reciprocal pronouns are:

| PERSON | SING. | PLU. |
|--------|-------|------|
| 1st | me | nous |
| 2nd | te | vous |
| 3rd | se | se |

The reflexive (reciprocal) pronoun of the third person is **se** for both singular and plural, masculine and feminine.

*B.* In form and function the reflexive and reciprocal pronouns are identical. In meaning, however, they differ. The reflexive pronoun indicates that the doer of the action of the verb is also the receiver or the beneficiary of that action.

| | |
|---|---|
| Il *s'*est vu dans la glace. | *He saw himself in the mirror.* |
| Ils *se* sont acheté des cravates. | *They bought ties for themselves.* |

The reciprocal pronoun indicates that two or more participants perform an action mutually upon each other.

| | |
|---|---|
| Ils *se* sont vus. | *They saw each other.* |
| Ils *se* sont donné des cadeaux. | *They gave each other gifts.* |

*C.* The disjunctive form **soi** is used only when the subject is one of the indefinite pronouns.

| | |
|---|---|
| *On* ne doit pas vivre pour *soi*. | *One should not live for oneself alone.* |

## 33. Special Uses of *Le.*

In French, **le** (invariable) may stand in place of an adjective, may summarize a whole idea, or may translate the English *one* or *so*. In many instances this use of le is pleonastic as compared with English. Some typical examples:

| | |
|---|---|
| Etes-vous content? — Je *le* suis. | *Are you satisfied? — I am.* |
| Venez, si vous *le* pouvez. | *Come if you can.* |
| S'il *le* faut, je lui parlerai. | *If necessary, I shall speak to him.* |
| Il est plus grand qu'il ne (*le*) paraît. | *He is taller than he seems.* |

NOTE: This use in comparative clauses is optional.

| | |
|---|---|
| Vous êtes Américain, et je *le* suis aussi. | *You are an American, and I am one too.* |
| Reviendra-t-il bientôt? — Je *l'*espère. | *Will he come back soon? — I hope so.* |

## 34. *Y* and *En.*

*A.* These words have the functions of both adverbs and pronouns. Their adverbial use is illustrated by the following sentences:

| | |
|---|---|
| **Il va** *à Paris.* — **Il** *y* **va.** | *He is going to Paris. He is going there.* |
| **Il vient** *de Paris.* — **Il** *en* **vient.** | *He comes from Paris. He comes from there.* |

The same sentences show the use of **y** and **en** as pronouns: **Y** replaces a phrase governed by **à** (**en, dans**), while **en** replaces a phrase governed by **de.** The use of **en** instead of a partitive noun was discussed in Chapter Two.

*B.* The uses of **y**:

1) As an adverb meaning *there,* **y** refers to a place already mentioned. The adverb **là,** *there,* usually refers to a place not previously mentioned.

| | |
|---|---|
| **Il est venu** *chez moi* hier, et il *y* est revenu aujourd'hui. | *He came to my house yesterday, and he came back today.* |
| **Mettez les fleurs** *là,* sur la table. | *Put the flowers there, on the table.* |
| **J'aime** *la campagne;* je m'*y* plais toujours. | *I like the country; I am always happy there.* |

2) **Y** is the pronoun that is used as a substitute for the preposition **à** (**en, dans**) + the name of a thing, an abstract noun, or a whole idea. Typical substitutions have been made in the following pairs of sentences:

| | |
|---|---|
| **Elle tient beaucoup** *à cette bague.* | *She is very fond of that ring.* |
| **Elle** *y* **tient beaucoup.** | |
| **Il se connaît** *en musique.* | *He is an expert on music.* |
| **Il s'**y** connaît.** | |
| **Je pense souvent** *à ce que vous m'avez dit.* | *I often think of what you told me.* |
| **J'**y** pense souvent.** | |

When the object of the preposition is a person, **y** cannot be used. It is replaced by **à** + a disjunctive pronoun.

| | |
|---|---|
| **Il pense souvent** *à ses parents.* | *He often thinks of his parents.* |
| **Il pense souvent** *à eux.* | |

*C.* The uses of **en**:

1) As an adverb meaning *from there*, **en** refers to a place already mentioned.

| | |
|---|---|
| **J'ai passé quelques semaines à New-York. — Tiens, j'*en* viens aussi.** | *I've spent several weeks in New York. — Why, I've just come from there too.* |

2) **En** is the pronoun that is used as a substitute for the preposition **de +**:

*a)* a noun used partitively referring to either persons or things.

| | |
|---|---|
| **Avez-vous *de* l'argent? — Oui, j'*en* ai.** | *Have you any money? — Yes, I have.* |
| **Avez-vous *des amis*? — Oui, j'*en* ai plusieurs.** | *Have you any friends? — Yes, I have several.* |

*b)* the name of a thing or a whole idea not used partitively. Typical substitutions have been made in the following sentences:

| | |
|---|---|
| { **Est-il coupable *de cette faute*?** <br> { ***En* est-il coupable?** | *Is he to blame for this blunder?* |
| { **N'avez-vous pas honte *de votre paresse*?** <br> { **N'*en* avez-vous pas honte?** | *Aren't you ashamed of your laziness?* |
| { **Vous souvenez-vous *de ce qu'il a dit*?** <br> { **Vous *en* souvenez-vous?** | *Do you remember what he said?* |
| { **Etes-vous capable *de comprendre cette leçon*?** <br> { ***En* êtes-vous capable?** | *Are you able to understand this lesson?* |

When the object of the preposition **de** is a person, **en** cannot be used. It is replaced by **de +** a disjunctive pronoun.

| | |
|---|---|
| { **Etes-vous fier *de vos parents*?** <br> { **Etes-vous fier *d'eux*?** | *Are you proud of your parents?* |

Despite this rule, **en** is frequently used in colloquial speech to refer to persons, especially with the verb **penser**. Thus, one hears:

| | |
|---|---|
| **J'ai fait la connaissance d'un de vos amis hier soir, et je vais vous dire ce que j'*en* pense.** | *I met one of your friends last night, and I am going to tell you what I think of him.* |

It would shock a Frenchman's ear, however, to make a similar substitution in the following sentence:

J'ai besoin *de mon frère* demain.   *I need my brother tomorrow.*

Therefore, it is obligatory to say:

J'ai besoin *de lui* demain.   *I need him tomorrow.*

### 35. Position of Conjunctive Pronoun Objects.

*A.* Conjunctive object pronouns immediately precede the verb that governs them. In compound tenses the object pronouns precede the auxiliary, since this is the living part of the verb. The only exception to this general rule is in the case of positive commands.

| | |
|---|---|
| Il *me* parle. | *He speaks to me.* |
| Il *m'*a parlé. | *He spoke to me.* |
| Il veut *vous* parler. | *He wants to speak to you.* |
| Ne *lui* parlez pas. | *Don't speak to him.* |
| Ils *en* ont acheté. | *They bought some.* |
| *La* voici (voilà). | *Here (there) she is.* |

*B.* In positive commands the object pronouns follow the verb. **Me** and **te** become **moi** and **toi,** except before **en.**

| | |
|---|---|
| Donnez-*moi* de l'argent. | *Give me some money.* |
| Donnez-*m'en.* | *Give me some.* |
| Assieds-*toi.* | *Sit down.* |
| Va-*t'en.* | *Go away.* |
| Montrez-*le-lui.* | *Show it to him.* |

*C.* Pronoun objects frequently occur in pairs. Theoretically, it is possible to have three pronoun objects together, but practically, such a construction is avoided. The following rules govern the order of the pronouns in pairs of pronoun objects:

1) Before the verb:

$$\left\{\begin{matrix} \text{me} \\ \text{te} \\ \text{nous} \\ \text{vous} \\ \text{se} \end{matrix}\right. \quad \text{before} \quad \left\{\begin{matrix} \text{le} \\ \text{la} \\ \text{les} \end{matrix}\right. \quad \text{before} \quad \left\{\begin{matrix} \text{lui} \\ \text{leur} \end{matrix}\right. \quad \text{before y} \quad \text{before en}$$

Eliminating **se,** which occurs less frequently in combination

than the other pronouns, the rule can be stated in a numerical
formula that is easy to remember:

    **1st** and **2nd** persons before **3rd** person\* before **y** (1 letter) before
**en** (2 letters); or:

$$1 - 2 - \overset{3\ *}{\underset{D-I}{\triangle}} - 1 - 2$$

    \* When both pronouns are of the third person, the **direct** object precedes the
indirect object.

| | |
|---|---|
| Il *me le* donne. | *He gives it to me.* |
| *Vous les* donne-t-il? | *Is he giving them to you?* |
| Il *le lui* a donné. | *He gave it to him.* |
| Ne *leur en* donnez pas. | *Don't give them any.* |
| Il *y en* a beaucoup. | *There are a lot of them.* |

    2) After the verb:

    **Direct object**  before  **indirect** object  before  **y**  before  **en**

| | |
|---|---|
| Donnez-*les-moi.* | *Give them to me.* |
| Donnez-*le-lui.* | *Give it to him.* |
| Donnez-*leur-en.* | *Give them some.* |
| Servez-*vous-en.* | *Use it.* |

## PART  II

### 36. Uses of the Disjunctive Pronoun.

The disjunctive pronoun is used:

    *A.* When the verb is not expressed.

| | |
|---|---|
| Qui avez-vous vu? *Lui?* — Oui, et *elle* aussi. | *Whom did you see? Him? — Yes, and her too.* |

    *B.* To give emphasis to subject or object pronouns.

| | |
|---|---|
| *Moi*, je ne l'aurais jamais fait. | *As for me, I should never have done it.* |
| Il ne me l'a pas dit, à *moi*. | *He didn't tell it to me.* |
| *Vous* aussi, vous avez eu peur. | *You too were afraid.* |
| *Lui* seul est venu; *eux* n'ont pas voulu venir. | *He alone came; they didn't want to come.* |

    Note: The normal conjunctive subject pronoun of the third person is
omitted when the disjunctive is used to emphasize the subject. This is not
true for the first and second persons, however, as may be seen in the group of
sentences above.

**C.** After ce + être.

| | |
|---|---|
| C'est (c'était, ce sera, etc.) *moi* (*toi, lui, elle, nous, vous*). | *It is (it was, it will be, etc.) I (you, he, she, we, you).* |
| Ce sont (c'étaient, etc.) *eux* (*elles*). | *It is (it was, etc.) they (masc. and fem.).* |
| C'est *moi* qu'il a vu. | *It is I whom he saw.* |

**D.** After all prepositions.

| | |
|---|---|
| Il court à *elle*. | *He runs to her.* |
| Ils sont chez *eux*. | *They are at home.* |

**E.** When the subject or object of the verb is double.

| | |
|---|---|
| *Vous et moi,* nous savons ce qu'il veut dire. | *You and I know what he means.* |
| Je vous ai vus, *vous et lui*. | *I saw you and him.* |
| *Son père et lui* sont partis hier. | *His father and he left yesterday.* |

NOTE: When the two parts of a compound subject are of different persons, they are summed up by a conjunctive pronoun subject that is in apposition with them. In the third sentence above, however, **son père** and **lui** are both of the third person, and so the summarizing conjunctive is unnecessary.

**F.** Especially with the verb **présenter**, *to introduce*, when the direct object is any pronoun other than **le, la,** or **les.**

| | |
|---|---|
| Nous *vous* présenterons à *eux*. | *We shall introduce you to them.* |
| BUT: Nous *vous les* présenterons. | *We shall introduce them to you.* |

## 37. Possessive Adjectives.

**A.** Table of the possessive adjectives:

| Person | Singular | | Plural |
|---|---|---|---|
| | MASC. | FEM. | MASC. AND FEM. |
| 1st Sing. | mon | ma | mes |
| 2nd Sing. | ton | ta | tes |
| 3rd Sing. | son | sa | ses |
| 1st Plu. | notre | | nos |
| 2nd Plu. | votre | | vos |
| 3rd Plu. | leur | | leurs |

NOTE: **Mon, ton, son,** are used instead of **ma, ta, sa** before a vowel or mute h: *mon* amie, *son* automobile (f.).

45

*B.* Possessive adjectives in French agree in gender and number with the thing possessed, *not* with the possessor. They must be repeated before each noun. English usage differs on both points.

| | |
|---|---|
| Marie a acheté *son* chapeau et *sa* robe dans ce magasin-là. | *Mary bought her hat and dress in that store.* |

*C.* In general, the uses of the possessive adjective are similar in French and English. Points of difference are:

1) In § 2 *F* it was said that the definite article replaces the possessive adjective before names of parts of the body, when there is no doubt about the identity of the possessor. The possessive adjective may occasionally be chosen to give extra emphasis.

| | |
|---|---|
| Il s'est cassé *le* bras. | *He broke his arm.* |
| J'ai mal à *la* gorge. | *I have a sore throat.* |
| Il l'a pris par *la* main. | *He took him by the hand.* |
| Il a ouvert *la* bouche. | *He opened his mouth.* |
| Elle a *les* cheveux blonds. | *She has blond hair.* |
| BUT: Je l'ai vu de *mes* propres yeux. | *I saw it with my own eyes.* |

2) Occasionally, the use of a definite article alone before the name of a part of the body might lead to doubt about the possessor. In this case, an indirect object pronoun is used to designate the possessor.

| | |
|---|---|
| Je *me* lave les mains. | *I wash my hands.* |
| La mère de la petite fille *lui* lave les mains. | *The little girl's mother washes the child's hands.* |

3) The possessive adjective is regularly used before the names of articles of clothing.

| | |
|---|---|
| J'ai mis l'argent dans *ma* poche. | *I put the money in my pocket.* |
| *Ma* robe vous plaît-elle ? | *Do you like my dress?* |

However, when the name of an article of clothing and the name of a part of the body occur in one sentence describing a condition, both are preceded by the definite article.

| | |
|---|---|
| Il est entré *le* chapeau sur *la* tête. | *He came in with his hat on his head.* |

4) When each of a number of possessors has but one unit of the thing possessed, the noun designating that thing possessed is singular.

| | |
|---|---|
| **Ils ont perdu *la tête.*** | *They lost their heads (i.e., each had but one to lose).* |
| **Quand ils veulent répondre à une question, les étudiants lèvent *la main.*** | *When they wish to answer a question, the students raise their hands, (i.e., each raises one hand).* |
| **Quand ils ont vu le revolver du bandit, ils ont levé *les mains.*** | *When they saw the bandit's gun, they raised their hands (i.e., each raised both hands).* |

5) Since **son** (**sa, ses**) may be ambiguous, **à** + a disjunctive pronoun are often added to make the meaning clear.

| | |
|---|---|
| **C'est *son* père *à elle* que j'ai rencontré. Je ne connais pas *son* père *à lui.*** | *It was her father I met. I don't know his father.* |

6) This same **à** construction may be used for emphasis. **Propre** also reinforces the possessive.

| | |
|---|---|
| **C'est mon idée *à moi.*** | *That's my idea.* |
| **Je l'ai vu de mes *propres* yeux.** | *I saw it with my own eyes.* |

## 38. Possessive Pronouns.

*A.* Table of the possessive pronouns:

| Person | Singular | | Plural | |
|---|---|---|---|---|
| | MASC. | FEM. | MASC. | FEM. |
| 1st Sing. | le mien | la mienne | les miens | les miennes |
| 2nd Sing. | le tien | la tienne | les tiens | les tiennes |
| 3rd Sing. | le sien | la sienne | les siens | les siennes |
| 1st Plu. | le nôtre | la nôtre | les nôtres | |
| 2nd Plu. | le vôtre | la vôtre | les vôtres | |
| 3rd Plu. | le leur | la leur | les leurs | |

NOTE: **Le nôtre, le vôtre,** etc., have a circumflex accent. **La leur** takes no feminine –e.

*B.* Possessive pronouns, like possessive adjectives, agree in gender and number with the thing possessed, not with the possessor.

47

Marie a acheté son chapeau à New-York; Louise a acheté *le sien* ici. — *Mary bought her hat in New York; Louise bought hers here.*

Quelle maison préférez-vous? — Je préfère *la sienne* (*à lui*). — *Which house do you prefer? — I prefer his.*

*C.* To express simple ownership, à + a disjunctive pronoun is used; to establish a distinction between possessors, the possessive pronoun is used.

A qui sont ces lettres? — Elles sont à *lui*. — *Whose are these letters? — They are his.*

Je vous défends de toucher à ces lettres. Ce sont *les miennes;* ce ne sont pas *les vôtres.* — *I forbid you to touch these letters. They are mine; they aren't yours.*

*D.* *A friend of mine* is translated idiomatically.

{ Un de mes amis.
{ Un ami à moi.

*A friend of mine.*

Un avocat de mes amis.

{ *One of my friends, a lawyer.*
{ *A lawyer, who is a friend of mine.*

# CHAPTER SIX

## RELATIVE PRONOUNS. NUMERALS. EXPRESSIONS OF DATES AND AGE

### PART I

### 39. Forms and Functions of the Relative Pronouns.

|  | Persons | Things | |
|---|---|---|---|
| Subject |  | qui | See § 41 A |
| Direct object |  | que | See § 41 B |
| Object of preposition **de** |  | dont | See § 41 C |
| Equivalent of **dans** (**à, sur, vers,** etc.) + a relative pronoun, to indicate place or time |  | où | See § 41 D |
| Object of all prepositions other than **de** | qui<br>See § 41 A | Masc.<br>Sing. **lequel**<br>Plu. **lesquels** | Fem.<br>**laquelle**<br>**lesquelles**<br>See § 41 E |
| Object of preposition without a specific antecedent |  | quoi | See § 41 F |

### 40. General Remarks on the Use of Relative Pronouns.

*A.* The relative pronoun, which is often omitted in English, must always be used in French.

| | |
|---|---|
| Le film *que* j'ai vu ce soir était peu intéressant. | *The picture (that) I saw this evening was rather dull.* |
| Le monsieur à *qui* vous avez parlé est mon oncle. | *The gentleman (whom) you spoke to is my uncle.* |

49

*B.* Relative clauses in French can never end in a preposition, as they so often do in English.

| | |
|---|---|
| **Le livre** *auquel* **je pensais s'intitule « Manon Lescaut.»** | *The book I was thinking of is called " Manon Lescaut."* |
| **La jeune fille** *dont* **nous parlions est ma fiancée.** | *The girl we were speaking of is my fiancée.* |

*C.* The relative pronoun agrees in gender, number, and person with its antecedent.  This affects the verb forms and the agreement of past participles.

| | |
|---|---|
| **C'est moi qui vous** *ai* **parlé.** | *It is I who spoke to you.* |
| **C'est nous qui l'**avons **vu.** | *It is we who saw him.* |
| **C'est vous qui lui** *avez* **parlé.** | *It is you who spoke to him.* |
| **Les fleurs que je lui ai** *envoyées.* | *The flowers that I sent to her.* |
| **Les livres qu'il a** *lus.* | *The books that he has read.* |

**41. Specific Uses of the Relative Pronouns.**

*A.* **Qui:**

1) **Qui** is subject of its clause (persons or things).

| | |
|---|---|
| **Mon ami** *qui* **est arrivé hier.** | *My friend who arrived yesterday.* |
| **Le tableau** *qui* **a été vendu.** | *The picture that was sold.* |

2) **Qui** is object of any preposition other than **de,** to refer to persons only.

| | |
|---|---|
| **Le professeur** *à qui* **j'ai remis mon devoir.** | *The professor to whom I handed my exercise.* |
| **La dame** *pour qui* **j'ai acheté ce cadeau.** | *The lady for whom I bought this gift.* |

3) Since **qui** does not show gender or number by varying its form, ambiguity may arise.  In this case, a form of **lequel,** which does change with the gender and number, is used.

| | |
|---|---|
| **La mère de mon ami,** *laquelle* **est arrivée hier, doit repartir demain.** | *My friend's mother, who arrived yesterday, is to leave tomorrow.* |

NOTE: In English, it is clear that the relative has *mother* as its antecedent.  In French, the construction of the possessive is such that the relative would seem to refer to the nearer noun, **mon ami,** if **qui** were used.  Hence the use of **laquelle,** which shows gender.

Le père de la jeune fille, *auquel* je vous ai présenté, est Français. / *The girl's father, to whom I introduced you, is French.*

NOTE: Here a similar situation is solved by the use of the masculine **auquel.**

In case both nouns are of the same gender and number, the forms of **lequel** are assumed to refer to the more remote noun.

### B. Que:

**Que** is direct object of its clause (persons or things).

L'homme *que* j'ai vu. / *The man whom I saw.*
La table *que* j'ai achetée. / *The table that I bought.*

### C. Dont:

1) **Dont** is *never* interrogative. It is the equivalent of **de +** a relative, to translate *whose, of which, of whom* (persons or things). The word order in a clause introduced by **dont** is normal, i.e.,

dont + subject + verb + direct object (if any)

Thus, the relative pronoun follows *immediately* after its antecedent. In English the noun after *whose* carries no article; in French this article must not be omitted. All these points are illustrated in the following sentences:

Madame Dupont, *dont vous connaissez le fils,* est arrivée hier. / *Mrs. Dupont, whose son you know, arrived yesterday.*
La lettre, *dont l'enveloppe est déchirée,* vient de France. / *The letter, whose envelope is torn (of which the envelope is torn), comes from France.*

2) A complication arises when the English *whose* precedes a noun that is the object of a preposition. In this case, French uses a form of **duquel** in place of **dont.** This rule may be stated as an equation:

| ENGLISH | FRENCH |
|---|---|
| **Preposition + whose + noun** | = **Preposition + noun + duquel, etc.** |
| *The tenor, **at whose concert** we were present, is singing again tomorrow night.* | Le tenor, *au concert duquel* nous avons assisté, chante encore demain soir. |
| *The street, **at the end of which** he lives, is very short.* | La rue, *au bout de laquelle* il demeure, est très courte. |

51

### D. Où:

1) **Où** is the equivalent of **dans** (**à, sur, vers,** etc.) + a relative pronoun, to indicate place or time. **Où** may have many translations, the most obvious of which are *where*, and *when*.

| | |
|---|---|
| La maison *où* je demeure. | *The house where I live.* |
| La maison *dans laquelle* je demeure. | *The house in which I live.* |

| | |
|---|---|
| L'heure *où* il est venu. | *The hour when he came.* |
| L'heure *à laquelle* il est venu. | *The hour at which he came.* |

### E. Lequel, etc.:

1) **Lequel** (**laquelle, lesquels, lesquelles**) is the object of any preposition other than **de**, to refer most frequently to things.

| | |
|---|---|
| C'est une chose *à laquelle* je ne veux pas penser. | *That is a thing that I do not want to think about.* |
| Voici un livre *pour lequel* je donnerai deux dollars. | *Here is a book for which I'll give two dollars.* |
| Je vais vous montrer l'Arc de Triomphe, *sous lequel* est enterré le Soldat Inconnu. | *I am going to show you the Arch of Triumph, under which the Unknown Soldier is buried.* |

NOTE: The use of **lequel,** etc. instead of **qui** to avoid ambiguity has been discussed in § 41 *A* 3.

### F. Quoi:

1) **Quoi** is used as the object of a preposition without a specific antecedent.

| | |
|---|---|
| Voici *de quoi* nous avons besoin. | *Here is what we need.* |
| Je sais *à quoi* il pensait. | *I know what he was thinking of.* |

These sentences are exactly equivalent to:

> Voici *ce dont* nous avons besoin.
> Je sais *ce à quoi* il pensait.

Both forms are equally acceptable.

2) Common expressions involving **quoi** are:

| | |
|---|---|
| Un je ne sais quoi. | *A vague something or other.* |
| Il a de quoi vivre. | *He has enough to live on.* |
| Il n'y a pas de quoi. | *Don't mention it (in response to proffered thanks).* |

## 42. Relative Pronouns with Demonstrative Pronouns as Antecedents.

In Chapter Three the fact was mentioned that demonstrative pronouns may be modified by relative clauses. Sentences of the types, *a*) *I know the one that you are thinking of,* and *b*) *I know what you are thinking of,* are a constant source of confusion. An efficient system for handling them will be described now.

STEP I: Decide whether the antecedent of the relative pronoun is to be a variable demonstrative pronoun (**celui, celle, ceux, celles**), or the invariable **ce.** How to make this decision is discussed in Chapter Three.

STEP II: Divide the sentence to be translated into its component clauses. If, as in sentence *b*) above, the word *what* is used, replace this word by *that which,* thus:

*a*) *I know the one* || ***that** you are thinking of.*

*b*) *I know ~~what~~ you are thinking of.*

   ***that*** || ***which***

STEP III: Determine how the verb in *each* clause governs its own object. In case of doubt consult Appendix IV. For example, in sentences (*a*) and (*b*), **savoir,** in the first clause, governs its object directly; **penser,** in the second clause, governs its object by the preposition **à.**

STEP IV: Translate each clause *separately,* paying no attention whatever to the second clause until the first is translated, thus:

*a*) *I know the one . . .*
**Je sais celui. . . .**

(Assume that *the one* represents **un poème**).

   *. . . that you are thinking of.*
   **. . . auquel vous pensez.**

(A form of **lequel** is used as object of the preposition **à.**)

*b*) *I know that . . .*
**Je sais ce. . . .**

(Here the word *that* represents no specific thing: hence, the invariable **ce.**)

   *. . . which you are thinking of.*
   **. . . à quoi vous pensez.**

(**Quoi** is used as object of the preposition here, since the antecedent is not specific.)

STEP V: Put the two clauses together:

*a*) Je sais celui auquel vous pensez.

*b*) Je sais ce à quoi vous pensez.

Another example of this technique:

To TRANSLATE: *He is trying to remember what he needs.*

STEP I: The word *what* does not refer to a thing previously mentioned. Neither its gender nor its number is known; hence, the invariable **ce** must be used.

STEP II: Division of the sentence into clauses:

*He is trying to remember ~~what~~ he needs.*

*that* ‖ *which*

STEP III: *Remember* = **se souvenir,** which governs its object by **de.**

*Need* = **avoir besoin,** which also governs its object by **de.**

STEP IV: Translation of *each* clause *separately.*

*He is trying to remember that* . . .
**Il essaie de se souvenir de ce** . . .

. . . *which he needs.*      (**Dont** is the relative pronoun that
. . . **dont il a besoin.**     is the object of the preposition
                **de.**)

STEP V: Combine the clauses:

**Il essaie de se souvenir de ce dont il a besoin.**

If the sentence had read: *He is trying to remember which one (the one that) he needs,* the antecedent of the relative pronoun would be referring to a specific thing, with gender and number known. Therefore, the French sentence would have read: **Il essaie de se souvenir de celui** (or **celle**) **dont il a besoin.**

54

## PART II

### 43. Cardinal Numerals.

| | | | |
|---|---|---|---|
| 1 | un, une | 41 | quarante et un |
| 2 | deux | 42 | quarante-deux |
| 3 | trois | 50 | cinquante |
| 4 | quatre | 51 | cinquante et un |
| 5 | cinq | 52 | cinquante-deux |
| 6 | six | 60 | soixante |
| 7 | sept | 61 | soixante et un |
| 8 | huit | 62 | soixante-deux |
| 9 | neuf | 70 | soixante-dix |
| 10 | dix | 71 | soixante et onze |
| 11 | onze | 72 | soixante-douze |
| 12 | douze | 80 | quatre-vingts |
| 13 | treize | 81 | quatre-vingt-un |
| 14 | quatorze | 82 | quatre-vingt-deux |
| 15 | quinze | 90 | quatre-vingt-dix |
| 16 | seize | 91 | quatre-vingt-onze |
| 17 | dix-sept | 99 | quatre-vingt-dix-neuf |
| 18 | dix-huit | 100 | cent |
| 19 | dix-neuf | 101 | cent un |
| 20 | vingt | 102 | cent deux |
| 21 | vingt et un | 200 | deux cents |
| 22 | vingt-deux | 201 | deux cent un |
| 23 | vingt-trois | 1000 | mille |
| 30 | trente | 1001 | mille un |
| 31 | trente et un | 2000 | deux mille |
| 32 | trente-deux | 1,000,000 | un million (de) |
| 33 | trente-trois | 2,000,000 | deux millions (de) |
| 40 | quarante | 1,000,000,000 | un milliard (de) |

The following points are worth noting:

*A.* The hyphen is used in compound numbers under 100 whenever **et** is not used.

*B.* Et appears only in **21, 31, 41, 51, 61, 71.**

*C.* The final consonant of **5, 6, 7, 8, 9, 10, 17, 18, 19** is silent before a noun beginning with a consonant only when the noun is multiplied by the numeral: six (*si*) livres. But: le six (*siss*) mai.

*D.* No elision occurs before **huit** and **onze**: *le* huit, *le* onze.

*E.* –s is used on multiples of **vingt** and **cent** when they are not followed by another numeral, **quatre-vingts, quatre-vingt-quatre, deux cents, deux cent six.**

*F.* Unlike the English, no article or numeral is needed to translate:

| | |
|---|---|
| *A (one) hundred (dollars).* | ***Cent** (dollars).* |
| *A (one) thousand (men).* | ***Mille** (hommes).* |

*G.* **Mille** is never pluralized.  **Million** and **milliard** act as nouns of quantity: they may be made plural and govern a following noun by **de**.

| | |
|---|---|
| **Deux** *millions de* **soldats.** | *Two million soldiers.* |

*H.* **Mille** becomes **mil** in dates.  Beyond **1100**, however, dates are usually expressed in hundreds, as in English.

| | |
|---|---|
| *Mil* soixante-six. | *Ten sixty-six (1066).* |
| *Quinze cent* quarante (or *mil cinq cent* quarante). | *Fifteen forty (1540).* |

*I.* The following collective cardinal nouns behave like other nouns of quantity (§ **8** *B* 1).

| | |
|---|---|
| *Une huitaine* de jours. | *About a week.* |
| *Une dixaine* de personnes. | *About ten people.* |
| *Une douzaine* d'œufs. | *A dozen eggs.* |
| *Une quinzaine* (de jours). | *About fifteen days, a fortnight.* |
| *Une vingtaine* (*trentaine, quarantaine, cinquantaine, soixantaine, centaine*) de dollars. | *About twenty (thirty, forty, fifty, sixty, a hundred) dollars.* |
| *Un millier* de soldats. | *About a thousand soldiers.* |

## 44.  Ordinal Numerals.

Except for **premier** and **second**, the ordinals are formed by adding –**ième** to the last consonant of the corresponding cardinal numeral.  **Cinq** adds **u**, and the **f** of **neuf** becomes **v** before the ending –**ième**.

| | | | |
|---|---|---|---|
| 1st | premier, première | 22nd | vingt-deuxième |
| 2nd | second(e) or deuxième | 71st | soixante et onzième |
| 3rd | troisième | 81st | quatre-vingt-unième |
| 4th | quatrième | 91st | quatre-vingt-onzième |
| 5th | cinquième | 101st | cent unième |
| 9th | neuvième | 1000th | millième |
| 11th | onzième | 1001st | mille et unième |
| 21st | vingt et unième | | |

The following points are worth noting:

**A.** Ordinal numerals precede the word they modify and agree with it in gender and number.

| | |
|---|---|
| Ce sont les *premiers* lilas du printemps. | *These are the first lilacs of spring.* |

**B.** In a phrase like *the first two (three)*, the cardinal numeral precedes the ordinal.

| | |
|---|---|
| Les *deux premiers* amis que j'ai vus étaient Jean et François. | *The first two friends I saw were John and Frank.* |

**C.** Premier is the only ordinal numeral that is used in dates and titles. *Second, third, etc.,* are translated by the cardinals **deux, trois, etc.**

| | |
|---|---|
| Le *premier* mars, Jacques *premier*. | *The first of March, James the First.* |
| Le *quatorze* juillet, Georges *six*. | *July 14th, George the Sixth.* |

**D.** Both cardinals and ordinals are used in speaking of the divisions of a book or play.

| | |
|---|---|
| A la page *un,* à la *première* page. | *On page one, on the first page.* |
| Chapitre *un* (*premier*). | *Chapter one (first chapter).* |
| Acte *I$^{er}$*, scène *I$^{ère}$*. | *Act one, scene one.* |
| Acte *deux* (*deuxième*). | *Act two (second act).* |

## 45. Fractions.

Regularly, the numerator is a cardinal, the denominator is an ordinal. Special forms are: **un demi,** *a half,* **un tiers,** *a third,* **un quart,** *a quarter.* The agreement of **demi** as an adjective has already been discussed (§ 27 *D*). When *half* does not modify a noun expressing time, weight, or extent of space, it is translated by **la moitié.**

| | |
|---|---|
| Le *tiers* de six est deux. | *One third of six is two.* |
| Le *quart* de vingt est cinq. | *One quarter of twenty is five.* |
| Deux *quarts* font *un demi*. | *Two quarters equal one half.* |
| *Cinq huitièmes.* | *Five eighths.* |
| Une *demi*-livre de beurre. | *Half a pound of butter.* |
| Une livre et *demie* de beurre. | *A pound and a half of butter.* |
| Une *demi*-heure; un mille et *demi*. | *Half an hour; a mile and a half.* |
| *La moitié* d'une pomme. | *Half an apple.* |

## 46. Simple Arithmetic.

| | |
|---|---|
| Trois et cinq font huit. | *Three and five are eight.* |
| Douze moins sept égale cinq. | *Twelve minus seven is five.* |
| Trois fois trois font neuf. | *Three times three are nine.* |
| Vingt divisé par quatre égale cinq. | *Twenty divided by four equals five.* |

## 47. Expressions Concerning Dates.

Quelle date sommes-nous aujourd'hui? (Quelle date est-ce aujourd'hui?) — Nous sommes (c'est) aujourd'hui le premier (le deux, le vingt-deux) mai.

*What is today's date? — Today is the first (the second, the twenty-second) of May.*

Quel jour sommes-nous aujourd'hui? (Quel jour est-ce aujourd'hui?) — Nous sommes (c'est) aujourd'hui lundi.

*What day is today? — Today is Monday.*

| | |
|---|---|
| D'aujourd'hui en huit (en quinze). | *A week (two weeks) from today.* |
| Dans huit (quinze) jours. | *In a week (two weeks).* |
| Il y a huit (quinze) jours. | *A week (two weeks) ago.* |
| Le mois dernier (passé); mardi dernier (passé). | *Last month; Tuesday last.* |
| Le mois prochain; lundi prochain. | *Next month; next Monday.* |
| Hier; avant-hier; demain; après-demain. | *Yesterday; the day before yesterday; tomorrow; the day after tomorrow.* |
| La veille; l'avant-veille; le lendemain; le surlendemain. | *The day before; two days before; the next day; two days after.* |
| Hier soir je suis allé au cinéma. | *Yesterday evening (last night) I went to the movies.* |
| Cette nuit je n'ai pas dormi. | *Last night I didn't sleep.* |

## 48. Expressions of Age.

Quel âge avez-vous? Quel âge a-t-il?

*How old are you? How old is he?*

| | |
|---|---|
| J'ai vingt ans. Il a trente ans. | *I am twenty. He is thirty.* |
| Il a dix ans de plus que moi. | *He is ten years older than I.* |
| J'ai dix ans de moins que lui. | *I am ten years younger than he.* |
| Un homme d'une cinquantaine d'années. | *A man in his fifties.* |

# CHAPTER SEVEN *

## INTERROGATIVE PRONOUNS AND ADJECTIVES. INTERROGATIVE WORD ORDER. EXPRESSIONS OF TIME AND DIMENSION

### PART I

### 49. Relative and Interrogative Pronouns *Qui* and *Que*.

Since students seem to have difficulty in distinguishing between the uses of **qui** and **que** as relative and interrogative pronouns, the following table is presented to refresh the knowledge already acquired about the relatives and to give the information needed about the interrogatives:

|  | qui | que |
|---|---|---|
| Relative pronoun | **SUBJECT** (persons or things) L'homme *qui* est ici. Le livre *qui* est là. | **OBJECT** (persons or things) L'homme *que* j'ai vu. Le livre *que* j'ai vu. |
| Interrogative pronoun | **PERSONS** (subject or object) *Qui* est entré? *Qui* avez-vous vu? | **THINGS** (object or predicate complement only) *Que* voyez-vous? *Qu'*est-ce? |

It will be seen at once that the relative **qui** and **que** are not differentiated on the same basis as the interrogative **qui?** and **que?**. As *relative* pronouns, **qui** is always a *subject*, while **que** is always an *object*, whether persons or things are referred to. As *interrogative* pronouns, **qui?** always refers to *persons*, while **que?** refers to *things*. This distinction is fundamental and must be thoroughly learned. By the use of these differences in function it is possible to build up, with positive assurance of correctness, the reduplicated forms of the interrogative pronoun.

**50. Reduplicated Forms of the Interrogative Pronoun.**

There are four of these forms, which may be broken down as follows:

| INTERROGATIVE PRONOUN | | | RELATIVE PRONOUN |
|---|---|---|---|
| 1) | qui | est-ce | qui |
| 2) | qui | est-ce | que |
| 3) | que | est-ce | qui |
| 4) | que | est-ce | que |

The *first* pronoun is the one that asks the question, the *interrogative* pronoun; **est-ce** never changes; the *second* pronoun introduces the second clause of the sentence and is, therefore, a *relative* pronoun.

To TRANSLATE: *What makes that noise?*

STEP I: The first pronoun is interrogative, and so the question is: Does the pronoun *what* refer to a person or to a thing? The answer is that it refers to a *thing*. Hence, by the table in § **49,** choose: **que.**

STEP II: **Est-ce** presents no problem, since it never changes.

STEP III: The second pronoun is relative, and so the question is: Does the pronoun *what* act as subject or object of its verb? The answer is that it acts as *subject*. Hence, by the table in § **49,** choose: **qui.**

STEP IV: Put the elements together, dropping the final –e of (interrogative) **que** (**qui** never loses its final –i under any circumstances):

*Qu'est-ce qui* fait ce bruit?

This same 4-step process may be used with any interrogative pronoun of this type. Of the four reduplicated forms, however, only the one that has just been worked out is obligatory. In other words, *what?* as a subject must be translated by **qu'est-ce qui?.** The simple forms may be substituted for the others as follows:

1) *Qui* est là?     instead of     *Qui est-ce qui* est là?
2) *Qui* voyez-vous?    instead of     *Qui est-ce que* vous voyez?
3) No substitution possible in *Qu'est-ce qui* fait ce bruit?
4) *Que* voyez-vous?    instead of     *Qu'est-ce que* vous voyez?

**51. Interrogative Pronouns as Objects of Prepositions.**

*A.* In the relative pronouns (§ 41 *A* 2 and § 41 *E* 1) **qui** was used for persons and **lequel** for things as objects of any preposition other than **de**. The relative pronoun that included **de** was **dont** (§ 41 *C*). In the interrogatives the situation is even simpler. **Qui?** is the object of *all* prepositions when reference is made to *persons;* **quoi?** is the object of *all* prepositions when reference is made to *things.*

| | |
|---|---|
| *De qui* parlez-vous? | *Of whom are you speaking?* |
| *Avec qui* partez-vous? | *With whom are you leaving?* |
| *De quoi* parlez-vous? | *What are you talking about?* |
| *Avec quoi* faites-vous cela? | *What do you do that with?* |

*B.* Since **dont** is *never* interrogative, a way must be found to translate the English *whose ?* This is done by the use of **à** or **de +** **qui?**.

1) **A qui?** indicates possession.

| | |
|---|---|
| *A qui* est cette maison? | *Whose house is that?* |

2) **De qui?** indicates relationship or authorship.

| | |
|---|---|
| *De qui* est-il le fils? | *Whose son is he?* |
| *De qui* est ce roman? | *Who wrote this novel? Whose is this novel?* |

**52. Asking for a Definition.**

To inquire about the nature of a thing or ask for a definition, **qu'est-ce que?** or **qu'est-ce que c'est que?** are used. The spelling of these forms is difficult and should be memorized.

| | |
|---|---|
| *Qu'est-ce que* c'est? | *What is it?* |
| *Qu'est-ce que c'est que* ça? | *What is that?* |
| *Qu'est-ce que c'est qu'*une mitrailleuse? | *What is a machine gun?* |

**53. Indirect Statements or Questions.**

Direct question:

| | |
|---|---|
| Qu'est-ce que vous faites? | *What are you doing?* |

A corresponding indirect question:

| | |
|---|---|
| Je lui ai demandé *ce qu'il faisait.* | *I asked him what he was doing.* |

61

A corresponding indirect statement:

**Je ne sais pas** *ce qu'il faisait.*      *I don't know what he was doing.*

The **qu'est-ce que?** of the direct question is reduced to **ce que** (invariable demonstrative + relative pronoun) in the indirect question or statement. Similarly **qu'est-ce qui?** becomes **ce qui,** and **qu'est-ce que c'est que?** becomes **ce que c'est que.**

| | |
|---|---|
| **Qu'est-ce qui** fait ce bruit? | *What makes that noise?* |
| **Je ne sais pas** *ce qui* **fait ce bruit.** | *I don't know what makes that noise.* |
| **Qu'est-ce que c'est** *qu'*une mitrailleuse? | *What is a machine gun?* |
| **Il ne sait pas** *ce que c'est qu'*une mitrailleuse. | *He doesn't know what a machine gun is.* |

A method of working out the correct translation for the combination of invariable demonstrative and relative pronouns was given in § 42.

**Qui?** and **quoi?** remain unchanged in passing from direct to indirect question or statement.

| | |
|---|---|
| { *Qui est-ce qui* **est entré?** | *Who came in?* |
| { *Qui* **est entré?** | |
| **Je sais** *qui* **est entré.** | *I know who came in.* |
| **A** *quoi* **pensez-vous?** | *What are you thinking about?* |
| **Je sais à** *quoi* **vous pensez.** | *I know what you are thinking about.* |

## 54. The Adjective *Quel?* and the Pronoun *Lequel?*

*A.* The usual confusion between these two forms may be easily avoided if it is remembered that **quel?** is an *adjective* and must therefore modify a noun with which it agrees in gender and number, while **lequel?** is a *pronoun* (agreeing with its antecedent in gender, but not necessarily in number) and can stand alone. Since both words translate the English *which?*, a simple trick may be used to differentiate the adjective from the pronoun: If the word *one* (*ones*) can be inserted in English after the word *which?* without destroying the correctness of the English sentence, the pronoun **lequel?** is the proper translation.

**Quelle maison a-t-il achetée?**      *Which house did he buy?*

NOTE: The word *one* could not be inserted after *which?*.

*Laquelle* a-t-il achetée ?      *Which did he buy?*

NOTE: The word *one*, inserted after *which?*, would not destroy the correctness of the sentence.

**B.** **Quel?** may be separated from îts noun by a part of the verb être.

| | |
|---|---|
| *Quel* est cet édifice ? | *What is that building?* |
| *Quelle* est la plus grande université du monde ? | *What is the largest university in the world?* |

**C.** **Quel !** translates the English *what a !* or *what!*.

| | |
|---|---|
| *Quelle* belle fleur ! | *What a lovely flower!* |
| *Quels* gentils petits garçons ! | *What nice little boys!* |

**D.** **Lequel?** implies that there is choice to be made between two or among several persons or things. **A** and **de** combine with the forms of lequel?: auquel, duquel, à laquelle, de laquelle, auxquels, desquels, auxquelles, desquelles. Lequel?, as well as the other interrogative pronouns, is always preceded by the preposition of which it is the object.

| | |
|---|---|
| *Lequel* de vos amis est venu avec vous ? | *Which (one) of your friends came with you?* |
| *Desquels* de ces livres avez-vous besoin ? | *Which (ones) of these books do you need?* |
| *Auxquelles* de ces revues vous êtes-vous abonné ? | *To which (ones) of these periodicals have you subscribed?* |

NOTE ALSO: *De quoi* parlez-vous ? *What are you talking about?*

## PART II

## 55. Interrogative Word Order.

There are three ways of making a declarative sentence interrogative: *A*) by prefixing **est-ce que**; *B*) by inversion of subject and verb; *C*) by a change in the inflection of the voice.

**A.** When **est-ce que** is prefixed to a declarative sentence, no change in word order is made.

| | |
|---|---|
| Ce livre est intéressant. | *This book is interesting.* |
| *Est-ce que* ce livre est intéressant ? | *Is this book interesting?* |

*B.* By inversion:

1) When the subject is a personal pronoun, or **ce, or on,** it follows the verb, to which it is joined by a hyphen.

| | |
|---|---|
| *Est-il* chez lui ? | *Is he at home?* |
| *Est-ce* vrai ? | *Is it true?* |
| *Parle-t-on* toujours de lui ? | *Do people still speak of him?* |

2) When the subject is a noun, a possessive pronoun, a demonstrative pronoun, or an indefinite pronoun, it precedes the verb and is repeated after it in the form of a pronoun.

| | |
|---|---|
| *Vos parents* sont-*ils* ici ? | *Are your parents here?* |
| *Les vôtres* sont-*ils* ici ? | *Are yours here?* |
| *Cela* est-*il* vrai ? | *Is that true?* |
| *Plusieurs* ne sont-*ils* pas partis de bonne heure ? | *Didn't several leave early?* |

3) Repetition of the noun subject in pronoun form is unnecessary when three conditions are met: *a)* the sentence must be introduced by an interrogative adverb (**combien, comment, où, quand**); *b)* the verb must be in a simple tense, i.e., present, imperfect, future, conditional, or past definite; *c)* the verb must have neither a direct nor an indirect object, nor a modifying phrase.

| | |
|---|---|
| **Comment va votre père ?** | *How is your father?* |
| **Combien coûte ce livre ?** | *How much does this book cost?* |

NOTE: It is not wrong, however, to say: **Comment votre père va-t-il ?**, and **Combien ce livre coûte-t-il ?**

*C.* Mere change in the inflection of the voice is sufficient to give interrogative value to a declarative sentence.

| | |
|---|---|
| **Vous ne partez pas ?** | *You aren't leaving?* |
| **Il est mort ?** | *He is dead?* |

*D.* Under certain circumstances the subject and verb of a declarative sentence are inverted, although the sentence is not interrogative:

1) When explanatory remarks are inserted into direct quotations.

| | |
|---|---|
| Je viendrai tout de suite, *dit-il,* mais je ne veux pas le voir. | " *I'll come at once,*" he said, " *but I don't want to see him.*" |

2) After certain adverbs or adverbial expressions.

| | |
|---|---|
| *A peine était-il* **arrivé.** | *Scarcely had he arrived.* |
| *Aussi suis-je* **venu.** | *And so I came.* |

Quite a few of these will be found in reading. They must not be translated as if they were interrogatives.

## 56. Expressions of Time.

| | |
|---|---|
| **A.** Quelle heure est-il? | *What time is it?* |
| Quelle heure avez-vous? | *What time is it by your watch? What time have you?* |
| Il est une heure; une heure et quart; une heure et demie. | *It is one o'clock; a quarter past one; half-past one.* |
| Il est deux heures moins le quart. | *It is a quarter to two.* |
| Il est deux heures cinq, dix, vingt, vingt-cinq. | *It is five, ten, twenty, twenty-five minutes past two.* |
| Il est trois heures moins vingt-cinq, moins vingt, moins dix, moins cinq. | *It is twenty-five, twenty, ten, five minutes to three.* |
| Il est midi; midi et demi. | *It's twelve o'clock (noon); half-past twelve.* |

NOTE: **Douze heures** is never used.

| | |
|---|---|
| Il est minuit; minuit et demi. | *It's midnight; half-past twelve.* |
| A quatre heures précises. | *At four o'clock sharp.* |
| Il est environ trois heures. | *It is about three o'clock.* |
| A six heures du matin; vers six heures du matin. | *At six o'clock in the morning; about six in the morning.* |
| A trois heures de l'après-midi. | *At three in the afternoon.* |
| A huit heures du soir. | *At eight in the evening.* |

**B.** Distinguish carefully between:

1) à l'heure and à temps.

| | |
|---|---|
| Je ne peux jamais arriver *à l'heure.* | *I can never arrive on time.* |
| Il est arrivé *à temps* pour prendre le train de neuf heures. | *He arrived in time to take the nine o'clock train.* |

2) en avance and de bonne heure.

| | |
|---|---|
| Quand j'ai un rendez-vous, je suis toujours *en avance.* | *When I have an appointment, I am always early.* |
| Je me suis levé *de bonne heure* ce matin. | *I got up early this morning.* |

65

3) **en retard** and **tard.**

| | |
|---|---|
| Je vous attends depuis dix minutes; pourquoi êtes-vous toujours *en retard ?* | *I have been waiting for you for ten minutes; why are you always late?* |
| Il est rentré très *tard* hier soir. | *He got in very late last night.* |

**57. Methods of Indicating Dimension.**

*A.* Notice the possible translations for:

1) *A mountain 12,000 feet high.*

Une montagne haute de 3600 mètres.
Une montagne de 3600 mètres de hauteur.
Une montagne de 3600 mètres de haut.
Une montagne d'une hauteur de 3600 mètres.

2) *The mountain is 12,000 feet high.*

La montagne est haute de 3600 mètres.
La montagne a 3600 mètres de hauteur.
La montagne a 3600 mètres de haut.
La montagne a une hauteur de 3600 mètres.

*B.* These phrases are also used:

| | |
|---|---|
| Ce jardin a *six mètres de longueur sur cinq de largeur.* | *This garden is twenty feet long by seventeen feet wide.* |
| Jean est plus grand que Jacques *de dix centimètres.* | *John is taller than James by four inches.* |

# CHAPTER EIGHT

## VERBS: THE PRESENT INDICATIVE, IMPERATIVE, FUTURE, AND CONDITIONAL

### PART I

**Foreword.**

Here begins a study of French verbs that will extend through Chapter Fourteen. The structure and function of the tenses, moods, and voices of the verbs will be examined, and special attention will be given to the idiomatic differences between English and French verb usage. A summary of what a verb is and does, and of the technical terms that are used in the study of verbs, will be found in § **V** of the Introduction.

### 58. General Considerations.

The indicative is the mood that is used to make a direct or indirect statement or to ask a direct or indirect question. It is found in both principal and subordinate clauses. Emphatic and progressive tense forms, found in English, do not exist in French. Thus, French has but one form: **je parle,** to translate: *I speak, I am speaking, I do speak.* In English, ellipsis of part of the verb is common. This is impossible in French. *He bought one, but I I didn't (buy one),* is translated: **Il en a acheté un, mais moi, je n'en ai pas acheté.**

### 59. Formation of the Present Indicative.

In regular verbs of the first (–**er**), second (–**ir**), and third (–**re**) conjugations, the present indicative is formed by adding appropriate endings to the stem of the infinitive. This stem is found by dropping the infinitive ending (–**er**, –**ir**, –**re**). The present indicative of irregular verbs may vary considerably from this pattern and should be studied in Appendix II. The regular endings are:

| PERSON | FIRST CONJUGATION | SECOND CONJUGATION | THIRD CONJUGATION |
|---|---|---|---|
| *Singular* | | | |
| 1st | parl–e | fin–is | vend–s |
| 2nd | –es | –is | –s |
| 3rd | –e | –it | –* |
| *Plural* | | | |
| 1st | –ons | –issons | –ons |
| 2nd | –ez | –issez | –ez |
| 3rd | –ent | –issent | –ent |

*Verbs of the third conjugation, whose final stem consonant is not –d–, add –t in the third person singular of the present indicative: **il rompt,** *he breaks.*

## 60. Uses of the Present Indicative.

*A.* In general, the present indicative is used to describe what is happening, or what is habitual or universally true.

| | |
|---|---|
| Il *fait* beau aujourd'hui. | *The weather is fine today.* |
| Il *vient* le dimanche. | *He comes on Sundays.* |
| Le travail *est* un trésor. | *Work is a treasure.* |

*B.* The present may replace a past tense to make a story more vivid (historical present), or it may replace a future to give a sense of immediacy.

| | |
|---|---|
| Il *accourt*, il *saute* sur le voleur, il le *saisit* au cou. | *He runs up, jumps on the thief, and grabs him by the throat.* |
| Je *viens* tout de suite. | *I'll come right away.* |

*C.* When the if-clause of a conditional sentence refers to future time, the present tense *must* be used. The structure of conditional sentences will be studied in more detail in § 65. For the moment, it is important to remember that the use of the future in an if-clause, common in English, is impossible in French.

| | |
|---|---|
| Si vous lui *donnez* cette somme, il pourra payer ses dettes. | *If you (will) give him that sum, he will be able to pay his debts.* |

*D.* The present is used to express an action or condition that began in the past and that is still going on or that has only just stopped. For instance, in the sentence: *How long have you been here?*, it is obvious that, although the condition began some time ago, it is still in effect. To translate this sentence, therefore, the present tense is used with the preposition **depuis:** *Depuis* **combien de temps** *êtes*-vous **ici?** The answer might be:

| | |
|---|---|
| Je *suis* ici *depuis* **deux jours.** | *I have been here for two days (and still am).* |

In other words, under these circumstances the French present tense translates an English present perfect tense. Other constructions are used in French to express the same time relationship: **il y a ... que, voici (voilà) ... que.** Questions may be asked by using **depuis quand?** and **depuis combien de temps?**

Examples of possible constructions:

| | |
|---|---|
| *Depuis quand* **nous** *attendez*-vous? | *How long have you been waiting for us?* |
| **Nous vous** *attendons depuis deux* **heures et quart.** | *We have been waiting for you since 2:15.* |
| *Depuis combien de temps* **nous** *attendez*-vous?<br>*Combien de temps y a-t-il que* **vous nous** *attendez?* | *How long have you been waiting for us?* |
| **Nous vous** *attendons depuis trois* **quarts d'heure.**<br>*Il y a trois quarts d'heure que* **nous vous** *attendons.*<br>*Voilà trois quarts d'heure que* **nous vous** *attendons.* | *We have been waiting for you for forty-five minutes.* |

These constructions are interchangeable, except that **depuis quand?** stresses the time when the action or condition began, whereas **depuis combien de temps?** stresses the length of time that the action or condition has lasted.

NOTE: This same principle applied to the translation of the English pluperfect is discussed in **§ 76 B.**

### 61. The Imperative Mood.

The imperative is used to give commands or make requests: *Leave the room; Please pass me the salt.* Its use in French is, for all practical purposes, similar to its use in English. The forms are those of the second person singular, first person plural, and second person plural of the present indicative, without subject

pronouns, however.  In first conjugation verbs, the –s of the
second person singular is dropped, except before **y** and **en**.

|  | First Conjugation | Second Conjugation | Third Conjugation |
|---|---|---|---|
| 2nd Sing. | parl–e | fin–is | vend–s |
| 1st Plu. | –ons | –issons | –ons |
| 2nd Plu. | –ez | –issez | –ez |

| | |
|---|---|
| *Parle* de ce que tu as vu. | *Speak of what you have seen.* |
| *Parles-en.* | *Speak of it.* |
| *Prêtes-y* toute ton attention. | *Give it all your attention.* |
| *Parlons* de votre travail. | *Let's talk about your work.* |
| *Parlez* de ce que vous avez vu. | *Speak of what you have seen.* |

## 62.  Forms of the Future and Conditional Tenses.

Except for some irregular verbs, the future and conditional
are derived by adding endings to the final –r– of the infinitive.

|  | Future | | Conditional | |
|---|---|---|---|---|
|  | Singular | Plural | Singular | Plural |
| 1st | vendr–ai | vendr–ons | vendr–ais | vendr–ions |
| 2nd | –as | –ez | –ais | –iez |
| 3rd | –a | –ont | –ait | –aient |

The future perfect consists of the future of the auxiliary verb +
the past participle of the verb to be conjugated;  the past conditional
consists of the conditional of the auxiliary + the past participle.

Future perfect:    **j'aurai vendu,** *I shall have sold.*
Past conditional:  **j'aurais vendu,** *I should have sold.*

## 63.  General Remarks on the Use of the Future and Conditional Tenses.

As in English, the future and conditional tenses are used as
follows:

| | | |
|---|---|---|
| *Future tense* | expresses | what will happen. |
| *Future perfect tense* | " | what will have happened. |
| *Conditional tense* | " | what would happen. |
| *Past conditional tense* | " | what would have happened. |

In addition, however, there are important idiomatic differences
between the English and French use of these tenses.  Therefore,
after examples are given of the " normal " uses, the following
points will be discussed:  1) the sequence of tenses in conditional

sentences; 2) the expression of volition; 3) the expression of habitual action; 4) the expression of implied futurity; 5) the expression of possibility and probability; 6) the expression of the future in reference to the past; 7) the expression of a deferential statement or request. If these discussions are to be understood, the student must dismiss from his mind the idea that *shall* and *will* always express futurity, and that *should* and *would* are sure signs of the conditional. It will become clear that these English auxiliaries must rather be translated according to the ideas that they convey.

## PART II

### 64. "Normal" Uses of the Future and Conditional Tenses.

FUTURE:

Je *viendrai* demain.                    *I shall come tomorrow.*

FUTURE PERFECT:

Je *serai arrivé* avant vous.            *I shall have arrived before you.*

CONDITIONAL:

Partir maintenant *serait* dangereux.    *To leave now would be dangerous.*

PAST CONDITIONAL:

Partir *aurait été* dangereux.           *To leave would have been dangerous.*

French makes a distinction between the immediate future and the absolute future that does not exist in English. The two English sentences, *He is going to explain it to us*, and *He will explain it to us*, are interchangeable. In French, however, the immediate future (constructed with **aller**) implies that the action will take place presently, whereas the absolute future implies that the action will take place either at a specified future time (no matter how near at hand), or at some unspecified moment in the future.

IMMEDIATE FUTURE:

Nous ne comprenons pas ceci; il *va*     *We do not understand this point;*
nous l'*expliquer*.                       *he is going to explain it to us*
                                          *(at once).*

ABSOLUTE FUTURE:

Nous ne comprenons pas ceci;             *We do not understand this point;*
1) il nous l'*expliquera* tout à l'heure  *he will explain it to us shortly*
(demain, lundi prochain).                 *(tomorrow, Monday next).*

71

2) il nous l'*expliquera*.          *he will explain it to us (some day, when he finds time).*

## 65. Sequence of Tenses in Conditional Sentences.

A conditional sentence regularly consists of two parts: 1) an if-clause, expressing a condition; 2) a result clause. Without becoming involved in a discussion of types of conditional sentences (contrary to fact, should-would, etc.), a simple formula for tense sequence will now be given:

| If-clause | Result clause |
|---|---|
| **A.** Present indicative | Future (sometimes Imperative or Present indicative) |
| **B.** Imperfect indicative | Conditional |
| **C.** Pluperfect indicative | Past conditional |

From this table two facts should be obvious: 1) If the tense of one clause is known, the tense of the other follows automatically (notice the perfect correspondence of tenses in English and French in the result clause); 2) A future, conditional, or past conditional is never used in an if-clause in French, despite the fact that they are so used in English.

EXAMPLES:

A. S'il *est* ici, je le *verrai*.       *If he is here, I'll see him.*
S'il *est* ici, *faites*-le entrer.       *If he is here, show him in.*
S'il *est* ici, je *vais* lui parler.       *If he is here, I am going to speak to him.*

B. S'il *était* ici, je le *verrais*.       *If he were here, I'd see him.*

C. S'il *avait été* ici, je l'*aurais vu*.       *If he had been here, I'd have seen him.*

When **si** means *whether* rather than *if*, it is followed by the tense required by the sense.

Je ne sais pas s'il le *fera*.       *I don't know whether he will do it.*

## 66. The Expression of Volition.

*Will* and *would* do not necessarily imply futurity or result.

72

Often they express volition and must be translated by the appropriate tenses of **vouloir**.

| | |
|---|---|
| Il s'intéresse à la musique, mais il ne *veut* pas venir à ce concert. | *He is interested in music, but he will not come to this concert.* |
| Il n'*a* pas *voulu* le voir. | *He wouldn't see him.* |

*Pres or Past*

### 67. The Expression of Habitual Action.

*Will* and *would* may also express habitual action in English. They are then translated by the present or the imperfect.

*Pres*

| | |
|---|---|
| Il *dit* souvent des choses qu'il ne croit pas. | *He will often say things that he does not believe.* |
| Le soir, il *fumait* sa pipe devant la cheminée. | *In the evening he would smoke his pipe before the fire.* |

*imp*

### 68. The Expression of Implied Futurity.

Frequently in English a present is used when a future is meant or a present perfect when a future perfect is meant. Under such circumstances French insists on using the tense called for by the sense. This is especially true after the conjunctions **quand, lorsque, aussitôt que,** and **dès que.**

| | |
|---|---|
| Je le verrai *quand* il *arrivera*. | *I'll see him when he gets here.* |
| *Dès que* vous *serez* de retour, faites-le-moi savoir. | *As soon as you get back, let me know.* |
| Faites ce que vous *voudrez*. | *Do what you like.* |
| Je resterai aussi longtemps que je *pourrai*. | *I shall stay as long as I can.* |
| Quand il *aura fini* ses devoirs, il ira se coucher. | *When he has finished his lessons, he will go to bed.* |

*happens*

### 69. The Expression of Possibility and Probability.

Idiomatically, French uses the future and conditional to express what is possibly or probably true, and to report hearsay information.

*F*

| | |
|---|---|
| Il *sera* deux heures. | *It must be two o'clock.* |
| Il *aura été* malade. | *He must have (has probably) been ill.* |
| *Serait*-il vrai qu'il soit parti? | *Could it be true that he has gone?* |
| A ce qu'on dit, il *serait parti* hier. | *According to rumor, he left yesterday.* |

*F Past* *Cond* *P Cond*

### 70. The Expression of the Future in Reference to the Past.

In indirect statements or questions, the conditional is used in a clause subordinate to a verb in the past tense.  This subordinate clause would have been in the future in the direct statement or question.  This should cause no difficulty, since the English construction is parallel.

DIRECT:

| | |
|---|---|
| J'*irai* avec vous, a-t-il dit. | " *I'll go with you,*" *he said.* |

INDIRECT:

| | |
|---|---|
| Il a dit qu'il *irait* avec moi. | *He said that he would go with me.* |

### 71.  The Expression of a Deferential Statement or Request.

In English the bluntness of a statement or a request is frequently toned down by the use of the conditional.  This is true also in French.

| | |
|---|---|
| Je *voudrais* le voir. | *I'd like to see him.* |
| INSTEAD OF: Je *veux* le voir. | *I want to see him.* |
| *Auriez*-vous la bonté de me prêter cinq dollars? | *Would you be good enough to lend me five dollars?* |
| INSTEAD OF: *Prêtez*-moi cinq dollars. | *Lend me five dollars.* |

### 72.  *Should* Expressing Duty.

*Should* is frequently synonymous with *ought* in English.  This meaning of *should* will be discussed in Chapter Thirteen as one of the idiomatic uses of the verb **devoir.**

### 73.  Spelling Peculiarities of First Conjugation Verbs.

Verbs of the first conjugation ending in **–cer, –ger,** and **–yer** or having the stem vowel **mute e** or **é,** show certain peculiarities of spelling that are phonetic in origin.  For a complete discussion of this question, see Appendix I.

# CHAPTER NINE

## VERBS: THE PAST TENSES. USES OF *MÊME* AND *TEL*

### PART I

**74. Formation of the Past Tenses.**

*A.* The imperfect indicative is formed, except in the cases of **avoir** and **savoir,** by adding appropriate endings to the stem of the present participle. These endings are the same for all three conjugations:

|  | SINGULAR | PLURAL |
|---|---|---|
| 1st | parl–**ais** | parl–**ions** |
| 2nd | –**ais** | –**iez** |
| 3rd | –**ait** | –**aient** |

*B.* The past definite is the fifth principal part of the verb; no general rule can be given for its formation. The endings of this tense for the three conjugations are as follows (note that the endings are the same for the second and third conjugations):

| PERSON | FIRST CONJUGATION | SECOND CONJUGATION | THIRD CONJUGATION |
|---|---|---|---|
| *Singular* | | | |
| 1st | donn–**ai** | fin–**is** | vend–**is** |
| 2nd | –**as** | –**is** | –**is** |
| 3rd | –**a** | –**it** | –**it** |
| *Plural* | | | |
| 1st | –**âmes** | –**îmes** | –**îmes** |
| 2nd | –**âtes** | –**îtes** | –**îtes** |
| 3rd | –**èrent** | –**irent** | –**irent** |

*C.* The compound tenses (past indefinite, pluperfect, past anterior) are formed by combining the proper forms of the auxiliary verb (**avoir** or **être**) with the past participle of the verb to be conjugated, as follows:

PAST INDEFINITE: present indicative of the auxiliary + past participle:

j'ai parlé, etc.                    je suis sorti, etc.

PLUPERFECT: imperfect indicative of the auxiliary + past participle:

j'avais parlé, etc.                 j'étais sorti, etc.

PAST ANTERIOR: past definite of the auxiliary + past participle:

j'eus parlé, etc.                   je fus sorti, etc.

### 75. Use of the Past Indefinite.

The use of the past indefinite belies its name. It denotes an action or a state that began and ended at a *definite* moment in the past. It may be the equivalent of an English present perfect (a form with *have*), in which reference to the present moment is implied. Or, it may denote simply a past event, or a succession of past events making up a story. Thus, the past indefinite is the narrative tense, answering the question, "*What happened?*" Most often it is used in familiar style, either spoken or written. The difference in use between the past indefinite and the past definite (the "literary" narrative tense) will be discussed in § 79.

| | |
|---|---|
| J'ai déjà *fait* tout mon travail. | *I have already done all my work.* |
| As-tu *vu* le nouveau film? | *Have you seen the new picture?* |
| J'ai *frappé* à la porte et il me l'a ouverte. | *I knocked at the door and he opened it for me.* |
| Le train s'*est arrêté* et Jean *est descendu* d'un wagon de troisième. | *The train stopped and John got out of a third class carriage.* |

### 76. Use of the Imperfect.

The several uses of the imperfect have one all-important element in common: they all represent actions or states that were in progress in the past. The imperfect is rarely used if any hint is given as to the time the action or state began or ended. Almost all the specific uses of the tense fit this general principle.

*A.* It has already been mentioned (§ 65) that the imperfect is regularly used in the if-clause of a conditional sentence when the result clause is in the conditional tense.

| | |
|---|---|
| Si j'*avais* dix dollars, j'*achèterais* cette petite table-là. | *If I had ten dollars, I'd buy that little table.* |

**B.** In just the same way as the French present indicative, used with **depuis** (**il y a ... que, voilà ... que,** etc.), translates an English present perfect to indicate that an action or state began in the past and is still going on (§ **60 D**), so the French imperfect, used with **depuis** (**il y a ... que, voilà ... que,** etc.), translates an English pluperfect to convey the idea that an action begun in the past was still going on at a later time.

| | |
|---|---|
| J'*étais* là *depuis trois jours* quand il est arrivé. | I had been there for three days when he arrived. |
| *Voilà deux ans que* je m'y *attendais.*<br>*Il y avait deux ans que* je m'y *attendais.* | I had been expecting it for two years (when it happened). |

NOTE: In this case the stress is on the description of what was going on when something else happened. Hence the imperfect, even though the beginning and end of the action or state are frequently well defined.

**C.** In indirect discourse, the imperfect replaces the present of direct discourse, when the verb of the principal clause is in a past tense.

DIRECT DISCOURSE:

| | |
|---|---|
| « Où *vas*-tu ? » m'*a-t-il demandé.*<br>Il me *demanda:* « Où *vas*-tu ? » | He asked me: "Where are you going?" |

INDIRECT DISCOURSE:

| | |
|---|---|
| Il m'*a demandé* où j'*allais.*<br>Il me *demanda* où j'*allais.* | He asked me where I was going. |

**D.** The imperfect is used to describe any state or condition that existed in the past, provided nothing is said about the time when it began or ended.

| | |
|---|---|
| C'*était* un grand jeune homme blond. | He was a tall, blond young man. |
| Le soleil *brillait* beau et clair. | The sun was shining bright and clear. |
| Elle lui a dit qu'elle ne l'*aimait* pas. | She told him that she didn't love him. |
| La maison du médecin *était* morne et délabrée. | The doctor's house was dingy and dilapidated. |

**E.** The imperfect also represents customary or repeated action. Again, such repeated action must take place over an indefinite period, and no beginning or end of this period may be mentioned.

| | |
|---|---|
| A l'armée, je *faisais* l'exercice tous les jours. | *In the army, I drilled every day.* |
| Quand il *faisait* beau, nous nous *promenions* au bord de la mer. | *When the weather was fine, we would stroll along the seashore.* |

*F.* Similarly, when two actions are represented as parallel, the imperfect is used, since nothing is known as to the beginning or end of the actions.

| | |
|---|---|
| Pendant que je *travaillais* en ville, il s'*amusait* à la campagne. | *While I was working in town, he was having fun in the country.* |

*G.* Finally, the imperfect is often used in narrative. Once again, the imperfect sets the stage for an action or describes what was happening when something else happened. In the following paragraph, the author describes how the old man *was sleeping*, how the little girl *was reading*, how the clock *was ticking*, when, at a definite moment, the narrator *entered* the room:

| | |
|---|---|
| Un bon vieux . . . *dormait* au fond d'un fauteuil. . . . A ses pieds, une fillette habillée de bleu . . . *lisait* la Vie de Saint Irénée dans un livre plus gros qu'elle. . . . La grosse horloge *ron⁹ait,* tic tac, tic tac. Au milieu de l'a⌐ ⁻upissement général, l'enfant *continuait* sa lecture. . . . C'est à ce moment que j'*entrai.* | *A good old man . . . was sleeping deep in an armchair. . . . At his feet, a little girl dressed in blue . . . was reading the Life of Saint Ireneus out of a book bigger than herself. . . . The huge clock was ticking drowsily, tick tock, tick tock. In the midst of the all-pervasive languor, the child was continuing her reading. . . . It was at that moment that I entered.* |

(Daudet, *Les Vieux.*)

This use of the imperfect is found in ordinary conversation in sentences like

| | |
|---|---|
| Mon père *était* assis à son bureau quand je *suis entré.* | *My father was seated at his desk when I walked in.* |

A sentence of this type follows the general pattern of those given in § *B* to illustrate the use of the imperfect with **depuis.**

## 77. Imperfect and Past Indefinite Contrasted.

The difference in function between the imperfect and the past indefinite should now be clear. To summarize:

Essentially, the imperfect is a background tense, setting the stage on which action is to take place. This background may be narrative, but it is narrative that describes what was happening when the really important event or events occurred. Thus, in the passage from Daudet, the significant action is the entrance of the narrator, not the things that were going on when he entered. In keeping with its character, the imperfect represents actions or conditions that existed over an indefinite period, whose beginning and whose end are unspecified.

Students frequently think that the duration of an action or condition in the past has something to do with the choice of tense. These two sentences will show that this is not true:

| | |
|---|---|
| **J'ai** *passé quatre ans* **en France.** | *I spent four years in France.* |
| **Ce** *matin-là* **il** *pleuvait* **quand je me** suis levé. | *That morning it was raining when I got up.* |

It is obvious that the past indefinite of the first sentence describes an action that is longer in duration than the one described by the imperfect of the second sentence. The conclusion, therefore, is that the nature of the action or state described, rather than its duration, determines the choice of tense. The action of the first sentence has a definite beginning and end; that of the second has not.

In § **76 E,** it was stated that the imperfect expresses customary or repeated action, provided the repetition took place over an indefinite period. The tense changes, however, when the period over which the repetition took place is limited.

| | |
|---|---|
| *Pendant mes trois ans de service à l'armée,* **j'ai** *fait* **l'exercice tous** les jours. | *During my three years of service in the army, I drilled every day.* |
| *L'été dernier,* **nous nous** *sommes promenés* **tous les jours au bord** de la mer. | *Last summer, we strolled along the seashore every day.* |

Finally, obscure situations may frequently be clarified by asking this question: *How often did it happen?* If the answer is: *Once,* the likely tense to choose is the past indefinite. Obviously, this formula will not work in the case of repeated actions, but in most other cases it will. It is offered as a convenient, although not infallible, rule of thumb.

## PART II

### 78. Use of the Past Definite.

The relationship between the past definite and the imperfect is parallel to that already discussed between the past indefinite and the imperfect (§ 77). In other words, a story may be told through the use of either combination. The past definite is also a narrative tense, and, like the past indefinite, it represents an action or state that began and was completely finished at some time in the past. The past definite is used to describe successive events in the following paragraph:

M. De Vornay *mourut*. Le père et la mère Nicouleau *moururent*. Le curé[1] *fut* plusieurs fois remplacé. Une crue[2] *emporta*[3] le ponceau[4] de l'Airelle, qui *fut* rebâti[5] en pierre. On *refit* la façade de l'église. D'humbles semis d'arbres[6] *devinrent* des taillis[7]; des bois *furent* abattus[8] et *découvrirent* sur le chemin des coins[9] nouveaux de l'horizon. Une maison *brûla*[10] au Prieuré. Mais, chaque dimanche, Pierre, Marguerite et Bijou se *rejoignirent*[11] devant le perron[12] du petit château. Marguerite, restée orpheline,[13] ne se *maria* point. Pierre ne *fut* point prêtre: on le *jugea* trop délicat de santé[14] pour entrer au séminaire. Laïque,[15] il *vécut* comme un abbé, dans le bien[16] que lui avaient laissé ses parents. Dimanches d'été, dimanches d'hiver, le temps *coula*.[17] La fine fleur de jeunesse se *fana*[18] sur le visage de Mlle de Vornay. Pierre se *voûta* légèrement[19]; mille rides[20] précoces[21] *sillonnèrent*[22] son front et le coin de ses yeux.                    (Prévost, *Le Pas Relevé*.)

[1] *priest*   [2] *flood*   [3] *swept away*   [4] *small bridge*   [5] *rebuilt*   [6] *saplings*   [7] *thick wood*   [8] *cut down*   [9] *corners*   [10] *burned down*   [11] *met again*   [12] *porch*   [13] *orphan*   [14] *of too delicate health*   [15] *layman*   [16] *property*   [17] *passed*   [18] *faded from*   [19] *became slightly stooped*   [20] *wrinkles*   [21] *premature*   [22] *furrowed*

### 79. Past Indefinite and Past Definite Contrasted.

Since the past indefinite and past definite are both narrative tenses, it is important to determine the circumstances under which each shall be used. It is not correct to think that the past definite is restricted to " literary " style, although it is sometimes called the " literary " narrative tense. It is frequently used in newspaper articles, or by public speakers to tell a sustained story.

The distinction between the two tenses may best be made from the point of view of the narrator. In general, the past definite is used to describe events in which the narrator had no personal part; that is, he neither witnessed them nor acted in them. The teller of the story quoted in § 78 had no connection with the events he described: he therefore used the past definite. On the other hand, the past indefinite describes actions or conditions in which the narrator had a personal interest. This explains why this tense is preferred for ordinary conversation and letter-writing. In the following passage, the story is being told by the author in the past definite, but in the conversation between the characters the past indefinite is used:

Son amie *poussa* un cri.[1]

— Oh !... ma pauvre Mathilde, comme tu es changée !...

— Oui, j'*ai eu* des jours bien durs,[2] depuis que je ne t'*ai vue*[3]; et bien des misères[4] ... et cela à cause de toi !...

— De moi ... Comment ça ?[5]

— Tu te rappelles bien cette rivière de diamants[6] que tu m'*as prêtée*[7] pour aller à la fête du Ministère.[8]

— Oui. Eh bien ?[9]

— Eh bien, je l'*ai perdue.*

— Comment ! puisque tu me l'*as rapportée.*[10]

— Je t'en *ai rapporté* une autre toute pareille.[11] Et voilà dix ans que nous la payons ![12] (Maupassant, *La Parure.*)

[1] *uttered an exclamation of dismay*  [2] *I have been through difficult times*  [3] *since I saw you last*  [4] *many hardships*  [5] *How is that ?*  [6] *diamond necklace*  [7] *lent*  [8] *ministerial ball*  [9] *What about it ?*  [10] *since you brought it back to me*  [11] *just like it*  [12] *but we have been paying for it for ten years*

## 80. Use of the Pluperfect and Past Anterior.

Both these tenses are translated by an English pluperfect. The French pluperfect is used much more frequently than the past anterior.

*A.* The pluperfect expresses what " had happened." As noted in § 65, it is found in the if-clause of a conditional sentence whose result clause is in the past conditional tense.

| | |
|---|---|
| Quand je suis allé la chercher, elle était déjà *partie.* | *When I went to call for her, she had already left.* |
| Si j'*avais eu* plus d'argent sur moi, je l'*aurais acheté.* | *If I had had more money with me, I'd have bought it.* |

*B.* The past anterior describes an action that is anterior to (earlier than) another past action. It is almost always used after conjunctions of time (**quand, lorsque, après que, aussitôt que,** etc.), and the action it describes was completed immediately before another began. As might be expected, the main verb of a sentence in which the past anterior occurs is in the past definite.

| | |
|---|---|
| *Après qu'il eut quitté* le village, il se dirigea vers la ferme de son oncle. | *After he had left the village, he directed his steps towards his uncle's farm.* |

### 81. Uses of *même*.

**Même** is used as an adjective, pronoun, or adverb.

*A.* **Même** = *same*, when it precedes its noun or when it is used as a pronoun.

| | |
|---|---|
| Le *même* fleuve; les *mêmes* choses. | *The same river; the same things.* |
| Il a choisi *les mêmes*. | *He chose the same ones.* |

*B.* **Même** = *self, very, even*, when it follows a noun or pronoun.

| | |
|---|---|
| Elle est la bonté *même*. | *She is kindness itself.* |
| Moi-*même;* eux-*mêmes*. | *I myself; they themselves.* |
| Les oiseaux *mêmes*. | *The very birds (even the birds).* |

*C.* As an adverb (invariable), **même** = *even*.

| | |
|---|---|
| Il a *même* refusé de partir. | *He even refused to leave.* |

### 82. Uses of *tel*.

*A.* As an adjective, **tel** = *such*. It is often used with the indefinite article: **un tel** = *such a*.

| | |
|---|---|
| *Telle* est l'histoire qu'il m'a racontée. | *Such is the story he told me.* |
| Je n'ai jamais vu *un tel* homme. | *I never saw such a man.* |
| On entend parler de *telles* choses. | *One hears of such things.* |

*B.* **Monsieur un tel** (**Madame une telle**) = *Mr. (Mrs.) So-and-So.*

*C.* When *such* is an adverb, it is translated by **si** or **tellement,** not by **tel.**

| | |
|---|---|
| Un *si* beau tableau. | *Such a beautiful picture.* |
| Un livre *tellement* intéressant. | *Such an interesting book.* |
| Le livre était *si* intéressant que j'ai passé toute la nuit à le lire. | *The book was so interesting that I spent the whole night reading it* |

# CHAPTER TEN

## AVOIR AND ETRE AS AUXILIARY VERBS. REFLEXIVE AND RECIPROCAL VERBS. AGREEMENT OF PAST PARTICIPLES. THE PASSIVE VOICE. SOME INDEFINITE ADJECTIVES AND PRONOUNS

### PART I

**83. Avoir and Etre as Auxiliary Verbs.**

*A.* **Avoir** combines with the past participle to form the compound tenses of all transitive verbs and of most intransitive verbs. Both **avoir** and **être** are conjugated with **avoir.**

| | |
|---|---|
| J'*ai eu* besoin de cela. | *I needed that.* |
| Il *a été* malade la semaine dernière. | *He was sick last week.* |
| Nous *avons vendu* notre maison. | *We sold our house.* |

*B.* **Etre** is used as the auxiliary to form:

1) The compound tenses of all reflexive verbs.

| | |
|---|---|
| Elle s'*est assise.* | *She sat down.* |
| Nous nous en *sommes allés.* | *We went away.* |

2) The passive voice.

| | |
|---|---|
| Elle *est aimée* de tous. | *She is loved by all.* |

3) The compound tenses of a few intransitive verbs and their derivatives that indicate motion or change of state. The list of these verbs may be more easily learned if they are arranged in groups of opposites.

| | |
|---|---|
| naître, *to be born* | monter, *to go up* |
| mourir, *to die* | descendre, *to go down* |
| | tomber, *to fall* |
| aller, *to go* | |
| venir, *to come* | entrer, *to go (come) in* |
|    devenir, *to become* |    rentrer, *to go (come) home* |
|    revenir, *to come back* | sortir, *to go out* |

| | |
|---|---|
| arriver, *to arrive* | rester, *to remain* |
| partir, *to leave* | retourner, *to go back* |

| | |
|---|---|
| Je *suis né* en 1918. | *I was born in 1918.* |
| Il *est mort* récemment. | *He died recently.* |
| Elle *est partie* hier. | *She left yesterday.* |

*C.* The verbs **monter, descendre, rentrer,** and **sortir** may also be transitive verbs. They then have the meanings: *to take (bring) up, to take (bring) down, to take (bring) in, to take (bring) out,* and they are conjugated with **avoir.**

| | |
|---|---|
| J'*ai monté* (*descendu*) ma malle. | *I took up (down) my trunk.* |
| Il *a sorti* les chaises. | *He took out the chairs.* |
| Il *a rentré* les chaises avant de se coucher. | *He brought (took) in the chairs before going to bed.* |

## 84. Reflexive and Reciprocal Verbs.

*A.* In § 32 the differences between reflexive and reciprocal pronouns were discussed. Using the definition given there of the functions of these pronouns, it is possible to define reflexive and reciprocal verbs: 1) a reflexive verb expresses an action that the subject of the verb performs, directly or indirectly, upon itself; 2) a reciprocal verb expresses an action that the individuals composing the subject perform mutually upon each other. The rules for the agreement of the past participles of reflexive and reciprocal verbs will be studied later in this chapter (§ 85).

| | |
|---|---|
| 1) Il *s'est levé.* | *He got up.* |
| Il *s'est lavé* les mains. | *He washed his hands.* |
| 2) Ils *se sont vus.* | *They saw each other.* |
| Ils *se sont parlé.* | *They spoke to each other.* |

*B.* Almost any transitive verb in French may be made reflexive through the use of a reflexive pronoun (*me, te, se, nous, vous*).

TRANSITIVE:

| | |
|---|---|
| La mère *a lavé* les mains de son petit garçon. | *The mother washed her little boy's hands.* |
| Elle *lui a lavé* les mains. | *She washed his hands.* |

REFLEXIVE:

| | |
|---|---|
| Elle *s'est lavé* les mains. | *She washed her (own) hands.* |

*C.* The conjugation of reflexive verbs is sometimes confusing because of the presence of two pronouns, one used as subject, the other as direct or indirect object. The full conjugation of **se laver** is given in Appendix I. The imperative (**lave-toi, lavons-nous, lavez-vous**) shows the object pronoun, but the imperative of the non-reflexive verb (**lave, lavons, lavez**) has no such object pronoun. The position of the object pronoun in the negative and interrogative forms of the verb should be noticed carefully.

*D.* In § 37 *C* 2 it was pointed out that the indirect object pronoun identifies the owner, when a definite article is used instead of a possessive adjective with the name of a part of the body. This indirect object pronoun is frequently reflexive and indicates that the possessor is performing an action upon part of his own body.

| | |
|---|---|
| Je *me* lave les mains. | *I wash my hands.* |
| Elle *s'*est coupé la main. | *She cut her hand.* |

*E.* Sometimes the reflexive suggests that an action is in progress, while a corresponding non-reflexive form describes the result of such an action.

| REFLEXIVE | | NON-REFLEXIVE | |
|---|---|---|---|
| Il se lève. | *He gets up.* | Il est levé. | *He is up.* |
| Il se couche. | *He goes to bed.* | Il est couché. | *He is in bed.* |
| Il s'assied. | *He sits down.* | Il est assis. | *He is seated.* |
| Il se meurt. | *He is dying.* | Il est mort. | *He is dead.* |

*F.* The replacement of a passive by a reflexive will be discussed later in this chapter (§ **86** *E* 2).

## 85. Agreement of Past Participles.

*A.* The rules for the agreement of past participles may be summarized as follows:

I. Agreement with the subject:

a) Verbs in the passive voice (conjugated with **être**).

b) Non-reflexive verbs conjugated with **être** (**aller, venir,** etc.).

II. Agreement with the preceding direct object:

Cl m'a blessé le bras
Je me suis blessé le bras

a) Verbs conjugated with **avoir.**

b) Reflexive verbs (conjugated with **être**).

EXAMPLES:

I.  a) **Elle *est aimée* de tous.**  *She is loved by all.*

b) **Elles *sont parties* ce matin.**  *They left this morning.*

II.  a) **Quels *livres* avez-vous achetés ?**  *What books did you buy?*

**Voici les livres *que* j'ai achetés.**  *Here are the books I bought.*

b) **Elle *s'est levée.***  *She got up.*

**Nous *nous* sommes *vus.***  *We saw each other.*

There are two common sources of error:

1) Since reflexive verbs are conjugated with **être,** it is assumed incorrectly that the agreement is with the subject.

2) In reflexive verbs it is sometimes hard to determine whether the reflexive pronoun is the direct or the indirect object. In the sentence, *She cut herself*, the reflexive pronoun representing *herself* is the direct object. Therefore there will be agreement of the past participle: **Elle s'est *coupée.*** But if the sentence reads: *She cut her finger*, the direct object is *finger*. The reflexive object must therefore be indirect (merely indicating the possessor), by the principle that a verb can have but one direct object, and the past participle will not agree: **Elle s'est *coupé* le doigt.** Sentences such as the following need special care:

**Les fleurs qu'elle s'est *achetées* sont très belles.**  *The flowers she bought herself are very beautiful.*

In this case the preceding direct object is **que** (referring to **fleurs,** fem. plu.), and **se** is an indirect object. The agreement is therefore with **que: *achetées.***

When the verb is intransitive, the reflexive object is obviously indirect, and there will be no agreement of the past participle. This may be seen in the case of the verb **se parler** (**parler** is intransitive, except when followed by the name of a language):

**Ils *ont parlé* à leurs amis.**  *They spoke to their friends.*

**Ils *se sont parlé* à voix basse.**  *They spoke to each other in a low voice.*

86

*B.* The past participle never agrees with the pronoun **en,**
except when an adverb of quantity precedes the verb.

| | |
|---|---|
| Avez-vous acheté des livres? — | *Have you bought any books? — Yes,* |
| Oui, j'en ai *acheté* plusieurs. — | *I have bought several. — How* |
| Combien en avez-vous *achetés*? | *many did you buy?* |

## *PART II*

### 86. The Passive Voice.

*A.* The passive voice consists of the verb **être** + the past participle of a transitive verb. The past participle behaves exactly
like any other adjective used after **être,** i.e., it agrees with the
subject.

*B.* Since the passive voice may appear in all tenses, the distinctions between imperfect and past indefinite, between imperfect
and past definite, and between past definite and past indefinite,
that were observed in active verbs, are equally binding in passive
verbs (§§ **77, 79**).

| | |
|---|---|
| Le soldat *a été blessé* dans la ba-taille. | *The soldier was wounded in the battle.* |
| La maison *était entourée* d'un jardin. | *The house was surrounded by a garden.* |

*C.* The agent (or doer) is preceded by:

1) **Par,** when a definite action is performed.

| | |
|---|---|
| L'enfant a été puni *par* son père. | *The child was punished by his father.* |

2) **De,** when a condition is being described.

| | |
|---|---|
| La maison est entourée *d'*un jardin. | *The house is surrounded by a garden.* |
| Personne n'est admiré *de* tout le monde. | *No one is admired by everybody.* |

*D.* In English it is possible to use the indirect object of an
active verb, or of an intransitive verb, as the subject of a corresponding passive verb. This is really a false passive.

ACTIVE: *John asks me the question.* (*Me* is an indirect object.)
TRUE PASSIVE: *The question is asked of me by John.*
FALSE PASSIVE: *I am asked the question by John.*

The false passive is impossible in French. It must be replaced by an active form whose subject is either a noun (if the doer is specified) or **on** (if there is no specific doer).

| | |
|---|---|
| *Jean* lui *a donné* le livre. | *He was given the book by John.* |
| *On* lui *a donné* le livre. | *He was given the book.* |
| *Plusieurs personnes* m'*ont parlé.* | *I was spoken to by several people.* |

NOTE: *To speak* is an intransitive verb in this sentence.

*E.* The passive is used less frequently in French than in English. It is commonly replaced by:

1) The corresponding active verb with **on** as its subject, when the doer of the action is not mentioned.

| | |
|---|---|
| *On a ouvert* la porte presque immé-diatement. | *The door was opened almost imme-diately.* |
| *On parle* français en Louisiane. | *French is spoken in Louisiana.* |

2) A reflexive verb, when the action is normal, customary, or possible (impossible) of accomplishment.

| | |
|---|---|
| Cette leçon *s'apprend* facilement. | *This lesson is easily learned.* |
| Les journaux *se vendent* partout. | *Newspapers are sold everywhere.* |
| Cela ne *se fait* pas. | *That isn't done.* |

No rule can be given that will define exactly when the **on** construction, rather than the reflexive, should be used to replace a passive. This is a problem for observation and discussion in an advanced course in French style, and it would be unprofitable to examine it in greater detail here. Notice that **on** may be translated by any of these English equivalents: *one, people, we, you, they.*

**87.** Uses of *autre.*

*A.* As an adjective.

| | |
|---|---|
| Nous l'avons vu l'*autre* jour. | *We saw him the other day.* |

*B.* As a pronoun.

| | |
|---|---|
| L'une est belle, *l'autre* ne l'est pas. | *One is beautiful, the other isn't.* |
| Quand vous aurez lu ces livres, je vous en prêterai d'*autres.* | *When you have read these books, I'll lend you others.* |

NOTE: The **d'** is partitive.

*C.* **Un autre** = *another (a different one);* **encore un** = *another (an additional one).*

| | |
|---|---|
| Ce chapeau ne me plaît pas. Veuil-lez m'en montrer *un autre*. | *I don't like this hat.  Please show me another one.* |
| Pourrais-je vous demander *encore une* tranche de pain? | *Could I ask you for another slice of bread?* |

*D.* **L'un** (l'une, les uns, les unes) is used in combination with **l'autre** (les autres) as both subject and object.

| | |
|---|---|
| *Les uns* sont partis; *les autres* sont encore ici. | *Some left; the others are still here.* |
| J'ai vu *l'un* et *l'autre*. | *I saw both of them.* |
| Je n'aime ni *l'un* ni *l'autre*. | *I like neither of them.* |
| Il n'a pensé ni à *l'un* ni à *l'autre*. | *He thought of neither of them.* |

*E.* **L'un** (l'une, les uns, les unes) is used with **l'autre** (les autres) to show reciprocity, provided the reciprocal pronoun is the object of a preposition.

| | |
|---|---|
| Ils étaient là *l'un près de l'autre*. | *There they were, one beside the other.* |
| Elles se souviennent *l'une de l'autre*. | *They remember each other.* |
| Ils parlent *les uns des autres*. | *They speak of one another.* |
| Ils se parlent *l'un à l'autre*. | *They speak to each other.* |

*F.* **Autres** is frequently added to **nous** and **vous** to emphasize the distinction between groups.

| | |
|---|---|
| *Nous autres* Américains. | *We Americans.* |
| *Vous autres* artistes. | *You artists.* |

## 88. Uses of *quelqu'un* and *quelque*.

*A.* **Quelqu'un** is an invariable pronoun meaning *someone*.  In the plural it has a masculine form, **quelques-uns,** and a feminine form, **quelques-unes,** and means *some, a few*.

| | |
|---|---|
| *Quelqu'un* est venu vous voir. | *Someone came to see you.* |
| *Quelques-uns* de ces jeunes gens sont assez intelligents. | *Some of these young men are fairly intelligent.* |
| Avez-vous jamais vu les belles plages de Californie? — Oui, j'en ai vu *quelques-unes*. | *Have you ever seen the lovely beaches in California? — Yes, I have seen a few of them.* |

*B.* **Quelque** (quelques) is the corresponding adjective.  It means *some, a few*.

89

| | |
|---|---|
| J'ai passé *quelque* temps en France. | *I spent some time in France.* |
| J'ai passé *quelques* années en France. | *I spent several (a few) years in France.* |

### 89. Use of *de* + Adjective after Indefinite Pronouns.

When an adjective is used to modify **quelqu'un,** *someone;* **personne,** *no one;* **quelque chose,** *something;* and **rien,** *nothing,* it is connected to the pronoun by the preposition **de.**

| | |
|---|---|
| J'ai fait la connaissance de *quelqu'un d'intéressant.* | *I met someone interesting.* |
| Je ne connais *personne d'aussi sympathique.* | *I know no one as likable.* |
| J'ai acheté *quelque chose de beau* ce matin. | *I bought something nice this morning.* |
| Je ne vois *rien d'intéressant* ici. | *I see nothing interesting here.* |

### 90. Uses of *chacun* and *chaque.*

*A.* **Chacun (chacune)** is a pronoun meaning *each one.*

| | |
|---|---|
| *Chacun* de vous aurait pu en faire autant. | *Each one of you could have done as much.* |
| Donnez une fleur à *chacune* d'elles. | *Give a flower to each of them.* |
| J'ai acheté des pommes à cinq sous *chacune.* | *I bought apples at five cents each.* |

*B.* **Chaque,** the corresponding adjective, means *each.* **Chaque** is singular and is used to stress the individual objects or persons of a group. **Tous (toutes) les** . . . stresses the group as a collection of individuals. This may be compared to the use of *each* and *every* in English.

| | |
|---|---|
| *Chaque* fois que je le vois, il m'ennuie. | *Each time I see him, he bores me.* |
| Il m'envoie un livre *chaque* année. | *He sends me a book each year.* |
| BUT: *Toutes les* fleurs ne sentent pas bon. | *Every flower doesn't smell sweet.* |

# CHAPTER ELEVEN

# VERBS: GENERAL CONSIDERATIONS ON THE SUBJUNCTIVE. THE SUBJUNCTIVE OF PERSONAL FEELING

## PART I

**Foreword.**

Many students seem to feel that they are getting beyond the elementary stages in their knowledge of French when they at last begin to study the subjunctive mood. This would suggest that the topic is at once of great complexity and of delicate subtlety. Actually, the subjunctive is put well towards the end of most French grammars not because of its greater difficulty, but rather because of its relative unimportance compared with other linguistic phenomena.

In the exercises based upon the first ten chapters of this book, many topics of current interest have been discussed with little use of the subjunctive. This demonstrates that it is almost always possible to express an idea in such a way as to make the use of the subjunctive unnecessary. Further, certain forms of the French subjunctive are now considered pedantic in speech and writing and are consciously avoided. It is true, however, that the mood is still very much alive in modern French, and the student must be able to use it in his own writing and interpret it correctly in his reading. Success in understanding the French subjunctive depends upon a grasp of the two basic principles that will be discussed in the next paragraph. Comprehension of these fundamentals should bring order out of the chaos of interminable lists of verbs, adjectives, impersonals, and conjunctions that do or do not " take " the subjunctive.

## 91. Significance of the Subjunctive.

So far, the ways of expressing simple statements of facts or commands have been discussed:

| | |
|---|---|
| **Il est venu me voir hier.** | *He came to see me yesterday.* |
| **Venez me voir demain.** | *Come to see me tomorrow.* |

The verbs have been in the indicative or imperative moods. But it may be desirable or important to give a different color to these statements of fact or commands, by stressing the speaker's personal feelings (joy, anger, sorrow, doubt, denial, etc.) toward the statement or command. Here, then, is one use for the subjunctive, which, in this case, might well be called the *subjective* mood. Again, while the speaker may often be sure of the past, present, or future reality of a fact that he is stating, there are times when it is desirable to present a fact as a mere possibility. This is the second use of the subjunctive. To summarize and illustrate these functions:

1) The subjunctive stresses the speaker's personal feelings toward the fact he is stating.

| | |
|---|---|
| **Je *regrette* qu'il ne *soit* pas *venu*.** | *I am sorry he didn't come.* |
| **Je *suis content* qu'il *fasse* beau aujourd'hui.** | *I am glad the weather is pleasant today.* |
| **Je *doute* qu'il *puisse* venir.** | *I doubt that he can come.* |

2) The subjunctive expresses possibilities as opposed to past, present, or future realities.

| | |
|---|---|
| **Je resterai *jusqu'à ce que* vous re-veniez.** | *I shall remain until you come back.* |
| **Travaillez ferme *de sorte que* vous *finissiez* bientôt vos devoirs.** | *Work hard so that you may finish your homework soon.* |
| **Il cherche *une maison* qui *soit* assez grande pour toute sa famille.** | *He is looking for a house that will be large enough for his whole family.* |

Upon these two fundamentals hang all the profits in the study of the subjunctive.

The discussion of the subjunctive will be divided into three parts: 1) ways of avoiding the subjunctive; 2) the use of the four subjunctive tenses; 3) the various uses of the subjunctive, grouped to illustrate the two principles just stated. The usual classification of the uses of the subjunctive (in noun, adjectival, and adverbial clauses) will be disregarded. It should be remembered that language is a spontaneous and occasionally erratic creation of the human mind; it may therefore be necessary to pull hard on some interpretations to make them fit.

An important point to begin with: The subjunctive occurs *only* in dependent clauses. Such seemingly independent expressions as:

| | |
|---|---|
| Vive le roi ! | *Long live the king!* |
| Ainsi soit-il. | *So be it.* |
| Qu'il parte. | *Let him go.* |

are really incomplete sentences whose principal clause (**je veux, j'ordonne,** etc.) has been lost.

## 92. The Avoidance of the Subjunctive.

*A.* The subjunctive is replaced by the infinitive when the principal and dependent clauses have the same subject:

1) After verbs like **vouloir, regretter, craindre,** etc.

| | |
|---|---|
| Je *veux partir.* | *I want to leave.* |
| Je *regrette* de vous *voir* ainsi. | *I am sorry to see you thus.* |
| Il *craint* de *se battre.* | *He is afraid to fight.* |

2) After expressions like **être content, heureux, fâché, surpris,** etc.

| | |
|---|---|
| Je *suis content* de vous *voir.* | *I am glad to see you.* |
| Il *est surpris* de nous *voir* ensemble. | *He is surprised to see us together.* |

3) After the prepositions **avant de, pour, afin de, sans** (if the subjects of the clauses are not the same, the subjunctive is required after the corresponding conjunctions **avant que, pour que, afin que,** and **sans que**).

| | |
|---|---|
| Il est venu me voir *avant de partir.* | *He came to see me before he left.* |
| J'étudie *pour (afin de) comprendre.* | *I study in order that I may understand.* |
| Il est parti *sans* nous *voir.* | *He left without seeing us.* |

*B.* When an expression of emotion (except fearing) governs a following noun or a pronoun by **de** (**être content de quelque chose, avoir honte de quelque chose,** etc.), the subjunctive may be replaced by an indicative through the use of the phrase **de ce que.**

| | |
|---|---|
| Je suis content *de ce qu'il est venu.* <br> Je suis content *qu'il soit venu.* | *I am glad he came.* |
| Elle est fâchée *de ce que je lui ai parlé.* <br> Elle est fâchée *que je lui aie parlé.* | *She is angry that I spoke to her.* |

*C.* When impersonal verbs like **il faut, il est temps, il vaut mieux, il est possible,** etc., refer to no specific person, the infinitive replaces the subjunctive.

| | |
|---|---|
| *Il vaut mieux travailler.* | *It is better to work.* |
| *Il faut manger* tous les jours. | *One must eat every day.* |

*D.* The subjunctive that follows some common verbs of commanding, permitting, and forbidding may be replaced by an infinitive. The noun or pronoun that would be the subject of the dependent clause becomes the object (direct or indirect) of the main verb. These formulae are useful and should be memorized:

**commander à quelqu'un de faire quelque chose,** *to order someone to do something*

**conseiller à quelqu'un de faire quelque chose,** *to advise someone to do something*

**défendre à quelqu'un de faire quelque chose,** *to forbid someone to do something*

**demander à quelqu'un de faire quelque chose,** *to ask someone to do something*

**dire à quelqu'un de faire quelque chose,** *to tell someone to do something*

**écrire à quelqu'un de faire quelque chose,** *to write to someone to do something*

**ordonner à quelqu'un de faire quelque chose,** *to order someone to do something*

**permettre à quelqu'un de faire quelque chose,** *to allow someone to do something*

**empêcher quelqu'un de faire quelque chose,** *to prevent someone from doing something*

EXAMPLES:

| | |
|---|---|
| Je *lui* ai demandé *de se taire.* ⎫<br>J'ai demandé *qu'il se taise.* ⎬ | *I asked him to keep quiet.* |
| Nous *l'*avons empêché *de sortir.* ⎫<br>Nous avons empêché *qu'il ne sorte.* ⎬ | *We prevented him from going out.* |

## PART II

### 93. Use of the Subjunctive Tenses.

The tense relationship of verbs in principal and dependent (subjunctive) clauses may be shown by means of a table:

| | When verb of main clause is **Present indicative Future Imperative** | When verb of main clause is **One of the past tenses Conditional** |
|---|---|---|
| When dependent verb is *simultaneous* with or *later* than main verb | 1) **Present Subjunctive** | 3) **Imperfect Subjunctive** (theoretically) |
| When dependent verb is *earlier* than main verb | 2) **Perfect Subjunctive** | 4) **Pluperfect Subjunctive** (theoretically) |

EXAMPLES:

1) Je *crains* qu'il ne *soit* ici.  *I am afraid he is here.*
   Je *doute* qu'il ne *vienne*.  *I doubt that he will come.*

2) Je *crains* qu'il ne *soit parti*.  *I am afraid he has left.*

3) Je *craignais* qu'il ne *fût* là.  *I was afraid he was there.*

4) Je *craignais* qu'il *n'eût été* là.  *I was afraid he had been there.*

The use made in these examples of the imperfect and pluperfect subjunctive is theoretically correct. However, in practice these tenses are avoided as pedantic. Only the third person singular is likely to be used, except in most formal style. In ordinary speech and writing, the imperfect and pluperfect are replaced by the present and perfect subjunctive respectively, unless the sense demands one of the past tenses.

Je *voudrais* qu'il *vienne* me voir.  *I should like him to come and see me.*
Je *craignais* que vous ne m'*ayez attendu*.  *I was afraid that you had waited for me.*

## 94. Use of Pleonastic *ne* in Subjunctive Clauses.

*A.* Pleonastic **ne** appears in subjunctive clauses introduced by affirmative verbs of fearing or by conjunctions of similar meaning. In this case **ne** does not negate its verb; it rather has the power to suggest misgiving, as does the English word *lest*.

Je *crains*⎫
J'*ai peur*⎭ qu'il *ne* vienne.  *I am afraid lest he come.*

95

Je suis parti $\begin{cases} de\ crainte\ que \\ de\ peur\ que \end{cases}$ vous   *I left for fear lest you see me.*
*ne* me voyiez.

    NOTE: Je *crains* qu'il *ne* vienne *pas*.   *I am afraid that he will not come.*

    *B.* Again, after affirmative verbs of preventing, with meaning similar to that of the English *lest.*

*Empêchez* qu'il *ne* parte.       *Prevent him from leaving.*
*Prenez garde* qu'il *ne* tombe.    *Take care lest he fall.*

    *C.* Pleonastic **ne** is usually found after the conjunctions **à moins que,** *unless,* and **avant que,** *before.*

Restez *à moins que* vous *ne* deviez   *Stay unless you have to go.*
   partir.
Parlez-lui *avant qu'*il *ne* parte.    *Speak to him before he leaves.*

## 95. Adjectives governing the Subjunctive of Personal Feeling.

    In all the subjunctives of personal feeling the stress is not so much on the statement of fact as on the personal comment that is made about it. This is seen very clearly in the nature of the adjectives (of pleasure, displeasure, surprise, regret, etc.) that govern such a subjunctive. Here are some of the most common:

Il est *heureux* (*content*) que vous   *He is glad you have come.*
   soyez venu.
Nous sommes *charmés* que vous   *We are charmed that you have come.*
   soyez venu.
Je suis *désolé* qu'il n'*ait pu* venir.   *I am sorry that he could not come.*
Etes-vous *surpris* (*étonné*) qu'il *soit*   *Are you surprised that he came?*
   venu ?
Je suis *fâché* qu'il *soit venu*.    *I am annoyed that he came.*

## 96. Verbs and Verbal Expressions governing the Subjunctive of Personal Feeling.

    Similarly, it is clear that verbs and verbal expressions of fear, regret, shame, doubt, astonishment, etc. should be followed by this type of subjunctive. Common examples:

Je *regrette* que vous *soyez venu*.   *I am sorry you came.*
Je *crains* (j'*ai peur*) qu'il ne *vienne*.  *I am afraid he will come.*
Je *doute* qu'il *vienne*.     *I doubt that he will come.*

*Vous étonnez-vous* qu'il *soit venu ?*  *Are you surprised that he came?*
*J'ai honte* qu'il *ait fait* cela.  *I am ashamed that he did that.*

NOTE: The subjunctive after verbs like **craindre** and **douter** might also be classified as subjunctives of possibility, for these verbs sometimes suggest that the fact mentioned is by no means certain.

**97. Impersonal Verbs governing the Subjunctive of Personal Feeling.**

Here again the stress is on the comment made about the fact stated.  Common examples:

| | |
|---|---|
| *Il est dommage* qu'il l'*ait fait.* | *It's too bad that he did it.* |
| *Il est honteux* qu'il l'*ait fait.* | *It's shameful that he did it.* |
| *Il est naturel* qu'il l'*ait fait.* | *It's natural that he did it.* |
| *Il est juste* que cela *soit arrivé.* | *It's right that that should have happened.* |
| *Il est heureux* que vous ne *soyez* pas *venu.* | *It's fortunate that you didn't come.* |
| *Il est bon* qu'il ne *soit* pas *parti.* | *It's good that he didn't leave.* |
| *Il est étonnant* qu'il *ait dit* cela. | *It is surprising that he said that.* |

**98. Conjunctions governing the Subjunctive of Personal Feeling.**

The two conjunctions **de peur que** and **de crainte que** obviously belong in this category, although, as in the case of **craindre,** the subjunctives that they govern might sometimes be classified as subjunctives of possibility.

**Je ne le ferai pas** *de crainte (peur)*  *I shall not do it for fear that he be-*
*qu'*il ne *se fâche.*  *come angry.*

*Je ne le ferai pas, pour de crainte qu'il ne se fâche soit fâché.*

# CHAPTER TWELVE

## VERBS: THE SUBJUNCTIVE OF POSSIBILITY.

### *PART I*

**Foreword.**

In Chapter Eleven, the subjunctive that registers a personal reaction to a statement of fact was discussed. The other category of subjunctives stresses the possibility, as opposed to the past, present, or future reality, of a statement. This chapter will deal, then, with things that " may possibly be," or that " may possibly have been."

### 99. Impersonal Verbs governing the Subjunctive of Possibility.

*A.* A number of commonly used impersonal verbs govern this type of subjunctive. Some of these expressions suggest the necessity or desirability of a future action:

| | |
|---|---|
| **il faut,** *it is necessary* | **il est important,** *it is important* |
| **il est nécessaire,** *it is necessary* | **il est temps,** *it is time* |
| **il est essentiel,** *it is essential* | etc. |

Others suggest mere possibility of such action:

| | |
|---|---|
| **il se peut,** *it is possible* | **il est douteux,** *it is doubtful* |
| **il est possible,** *it is possible* | **il semble,** *it seems* |
| | etc. |

EXAMPLES:

| | |
|---|---|
| *Il était temps* **qu'il s'en** *allât.* | { *It was time that he went.* <br> { *It was time for him to go.* |
| *Il semble* **qu'il** *ait pu* **venir.** | *It seems that he could have come.* |
| *Il faut* **que vous** *partiez.* | *You must leave.* |

NOTE: With **falloir,** the pronoun subject of a dependent clause may become the indirect object of **falloir.** The subjunctive is then replaced by an infinitive: Il *vous* **faut** *partir.*

*B.* The suggestion of mere possibility in these impersonals may be more clearly seen, if they are contrasted with a group of

98

impersonals that govern the indicative. **Il est possible** hints that something may or may not happen and governs a subjunctive; but **il est probable** stresses the greater likelihood of some future development and so governs the indicative. **Il semble** is a weak statement of possibility and governs the subjunctive; but **il me semble** stresses personal conviction on the part of the speaker and so governs the indicative. A suggestive list of impersonals governing the indicative follows:

| | |
|---|---|
| **il est sûr,** *it is sure* | **il est probable,** *it is probable* |
| **il est certain,** *it is certain* | **il me semble,** *it seems to me* |
| **il est évident,** *it is evident* | **il paraît,** *it appears, it is evident* |
| **il est clair,** *it is clear* | etc. |

EXAMPLES:

| | |
|---|---|
| *Il est évident* qu'il ne *peut* pas partir. | *It is evident that he cannot leave.* |
| *Il me semble* que vous ne *travaillez* pas assez. | *It seems to me that you do not work hard enough.* |
| *Il était certain* qu'il *était* malade. | *It was certain that he was ill.* |

Just as logically, if these expressions of greater certainty are used negatively or interrogatively, they immediately cast doubt on the reality of the statement that they govern. The indicative is then abandoned in favor of the subjunctive.

| | |
|---|---|
| *Il ne me semble pas* qu'il *ait pu* faire cela. | *It doesn't seem to me that he could have done that.* |
| *Est-il certain* qu'il *soit venu?* | *Is it certain that he has come?* |

## 100. Personal Verbs governing the Subjunctive of Possibility.

Such verbs fall more or less into two groups, both of which look toward unattained future actions. One group suggests wishing or preferring:

| | |
|---|---|
| **vouloir,** *to wish, want* | **préférer,** *to prefer* |
| **désirer,** *to desire* | **aimer mieux,** *to prefer* |
| **souhaiter,** *to wish* | etc. |

The other group suggests the issuing of orders, permission, or prohibitions:

| | | | |
|---|---|---|---|
| **demander,** *to ask* | **consentir,** *to consent* | **dire** | (in the sense of *tell* |
| **ordonner,** *to order* | **empêcher,** *to prevent* | **écrire** | [*write*] *someone* |
| **permettre,** *to permit* | **défendre,** *to forbid* | etc. | *to do something.*) |

99

EXAMPLES:

| | |
|---|---|
| Je *préférais* qu'il s'en *allât*. | *I preferred that he go away.* |
| *Empêchez* qu'il ne *sorte*. | *Prevent him from going out.* |
| Il *a consenti* (à ce) que nous *partions*. | *He consented to our leaving.* |
| Je *voudrais* que vous me *donniez* cela. | *I would like you to give me that.* |

NOTE: When the subject of **vouloir** is different from that of the dependent verb, it is impossible to use an infinitive construction as is done in English.

**101. Clauses governed by *croire, penser,* and *espérer*.**

*A.* These three troublesome verbs deserve a paragraph all to themselves. In the affirmative they convey a strong belief in the reality or fulfillment of the statement that they govern, which, therefore, appears in the indicative.

| | |
|---|---|
| Je *crois* qu'il *est* honnête. | *I believe he is honest.* |
| J'*espère* que vous *viendrez* avec nous. | *I hope that you will come with us.* |
| Je *pensais* qu'il *serait* ici. | *I thought that he would be here.* |
| Je *croyais* qu'il *était venu*. | *I thought he had come.* |

*B.* As in the case of impersonals like **il est certain**, it is logical enough to assume that **croire, penser,** and **espérer** will lose the indicative and adopt the subjunctive when they become negative or interrogative.

| | |
|---|---|
| Je *ne crois pas* qu'il *soit venu*. | *I don't think he came.* |
| Il *n'espère plus* que son père *soit* vivant. | *He no longer hopes that his father is alive.* |
| *Croyez-vous* qu'il *sache* de quoi il s'agit? | *Do you think he knows what it is all about?* |

EXCEPTIONS:

1) When these verbs are interrogative and refer to future time, they are followed by the future or conditional.

| | |
|---|---|
| *Croyez-vous* qu'il *partira* demain? | *Do you think he will leave tomorrow?* |
| *Espérez-vous* qu'il *reviendra*? | *Do you hope he'll come back?* |
| *Espériez-vous* qu'il *reviendrait*? | *Were you hoping he would come back?* |

2) When these verbs are negative in a past tense and refer to future time, they are followed by the conditional.

100

| | |
|---|---|
| Je *ne pensais pas* qu'il me *parlerait*. | *I didn't think he would speak to me.* |
| Vraiment, je *n'espérais pas* que vous me *donneriez* tant d'argent. | *I didn't really hope that you would give me so much money.* |

## PART II

**102. Conjunctions governing the Subjunctive of Possibility.**

The conjunctions that govern the subjunctive either look forward to future action or express mental reservation, thereby suggesting uncertainty. They may be divided into groups:

*A.* Conjunctions pointing toward future time:

avant que, *before*
jusqu'à ce que, *until*

| | |
|---|---|
| Je ne partirai pas *avant qu'*il *revienne*. | *I shall not leave until he gets back.* |
| Je resterai *jusqu'à ce qu'*il *arrive*. | *I shall remain until he gets here.* |

Add to these the verb **attendre,** *to wait:*

| | |
|---|---|
| *Attendez qu'*il *revienne*. | *Wait till he gets back.* |

*B.* Conjunctions expressing purpose:

pour que ⎱, *in order that*
afin que ⎰

de sorte que ⎫
de façon que ⎬, *so that*
de manière que ⎭

| | |
|---|---|
| Je vous écris *pour que* (*afin que*) vous *sachiez* ce que j'en pense. | *I am writing you in order that you may know what I think of it.* |
| Travaillez ferme *de sorte que* vous *puissiez* nous accompagner. | *Work hard so that you may go with us.* |

When **de sorte que, de façon que,** and **de manière que** express accomplished result rather than purpose for the future, they are followed by the indicative, as would seem quite natural.

| | |
|---|---|
| Il a travaillé ferme *de sorte qu'*il *a pu* nous accompagner. | *He worked hard so that he was able to go with us.* |

*C.* Conjunctions expressing mental reservation, and suggesting hesitation or uncertainty:

à moins que, *unless*       quoique ⎱, *although*
pourvu que, *provided that*   bien que ⎰

| | |
|---|---|
| Je ne partirai pas *à moins que* vous ne *partiez* aussi. | *I shall not leave unless you leave too.* |
| Je partirai *pourvu que* vous *partiez* aussi. | *I shall leave provided that you leave too.* |
| *Quoique* (*bien que*) vous ne *partiez* pas, je sens que vous en avez le désir. | *Although you are not leaving, I feel that you want to.* |

    *D.* The conjunction of negation: **sans que,** *without.*

| | |
|---|---|
| Il est parti *sans que* je le *voie* (*sans que* je le *visse*). | *He left without my seeing him.* |

## 103. Vague, Non-existent, or Exaggerated Antecedents governing the Subjunctive of Possibility.

    *A.* The subjunctive is used in a dependent adjectival clause modifying a noun whose existence is not yet a reality. This is sometimes called " the subjunctive describing a characteristic sought for, but not yet found." Once the desired characteristic has been found, however, the verb describing it will be in the indicative.

| | |
|---|---|
| Connaissez-vous *un roman moderne* qui *soit* vraiment bien écrit? | *Do you know a modern novel that is really well written?* |
| Je cherche *une maison* qui *soit* assez grande pour toute ma famille. | *I am looking for a house that will be large enough for my whole family.* |

    In the following sentence the characteristic has been found· hence, the indicative:

| | |
|---|---|
| J'ai trouvé *une maison* qui *est* assez grande pour toute ma famille. | *I have found a house that is large enough for my whole family* |

    *B.* Sometimes the antecedent is a negative or is used with a negative verb. This amounts to denying the existence of the antecedent, and it is natural to look for a subjunctive in the modifying clause.

| | |
|---|---|
| Je *ne connais personne* qui *soit* aussi intelligent que lui. | *I know no one who is as intelligent as he.* |
| Il *n'y a rien* qui *soit* plus à désirer. | *There is nothing that is more to be desired.* |

102

*Il n'y a pas de raison* qu'il *puisse*   *There is no reason that he can give.*
donner.

**C.** Similarly, the antecedent may be modified by a superlative adjective or by **seul, premier,** or **dernier,** which have the
force of superlatives. Such superlatives are usually exaggerations,
and this lack of reality is reflected in the subjunctive of the dependent adjectival clause. Of course, when **seul, premier,** and **dernier**
can be taken literally, the modifying clause has an indicative verb.

C'est *le plus beau parc* que j'aie ja-   *This is the loveliest park I have ever*
mais *vu.*   *seen.*
C'est *le seul ami* que j'*aie.*   *He is the only friend I have.*
C'est *la dernière fois* que je *sorte*   *This is the last time I'll go out with*
avec vous.   *you.*

But, when a fact is stated:

C'est *le seul livre* que j'*ai.*   *This is the only book I have.*
*La dernière fois* que je l'*ai vu,* nous   *The last time I saw him, we went*
sommes allés au cinéma.   *to the movies.*

**D.** The addition of *–ever* to the English words *who, what,
how,* and *where* gives them an indefinite meaning. Consequently,
a clause modifying such an indefinite antecedent will be in the subjunctive. These constructions will be the more readily understood
if they are divided into their component parts: an indefinite word,
and a dependent adjectival clause in the subjunctive.

1) WHOEVER:

*Qui* que vous *soyez* . . .   *Whoever you may be* . . .

2) WHATEVER (pronoun):

*Quoi* que vous *disiez* . . .   *Whatever you may say* . . .

3) WHATEVER (predicate adjective):

*Quelles* que *soient* vos raisons . . .   *Whatever your reasons may be* . . .

NOTE: By the inversion of subject and verb, the verb is kept away from
the end of the clause. This is considered better style in French.

4) WHATEVER (attributive adjective):

*Quelques* livres qu'il *lise* . . .   *Whatever books he may read* . . .

5) HOWEVER (adverb):

*Quelque* intelligent qu'il *soit* ...          *However intelligent he may be* ...
*Quelque* rapidement qu'il le          *However rapidly he may do it* ...
*fasse* ...

6) WHEREVER:

*Où* qu'on *aille* ...          *Wherever one may go* ...

**104. A Note on *que*.**

The conjunction **que** may be followed by either the indicative or the subjunctive. It may not be omitted in French, as it frequently is in English. To avoid repetition of other conjunctions, **que** may be used. When it is so used, it is followed by the same construction as the conjunction that it replaces, except that when **que** stands instead of **si**, *if*, it is followed by a subjunctive.

Je crois *qu*'il le fera.          *I think (that) he will do it.*
Nous irons au théâtre ensemble, *quand* vous *aurez* le temps et *que* j'*aurai* assez d'argent.          *We'll go to the theater together, when you have the time and (when) I have enough money.*
*Si* vous *avez* le temps, et *que* j'*aie* assez d'argent, nous irons au théâtre ensemble.          *If you have the time, and (if) I have enough money, we'll go to the theater together.*

# CHAPTER THIRTEEN

## VERBS: IMPERSONAL VERBS. USES OF *FALLOIR, DEVOIR, VOULOIR, POUVOIR, SAVOIR, LAISSER, FAIRE*. USES OF *N'IMPORTE QUI*

### *PART I*

**105. Forms and Uses of Impersonal Verbs.**

*A.* An impersonal verb is one that is conjugated in the third person singular only. The subject is always **il,** *it, there.* Some impersonals are regularly conjugated, others irregularly. Verbs describing weather and denoting time are impersonal, as in English.

| | |
|---|---|
| **Il pleut; il neigera; il a gelé hier.** | *It is raining; it will snow; it froze yesterday.* |
| **Il fait beau; il fait froid.** | *It is fine weather; it is cold.* |
| **Il est deux heures; il est tard.** | *It is two o'clock; it is late.* |

*B.* **Y avoir** is one of the commonest of impersonals and is used in all tenses.

| | |
|---|---|
| **Il y a; il y a eu; il y aura, etc.** | *There is (are); there has (have) been; there will be, etc.* |

**Voilà,** *there is, there are* differs in use from **il y a.** The former is demonstrative, pointing out an object and answering the question *where is?* or *where are?* **Il y a,** however, makes a general statement. without demonstrative force.

| | |
|---|---|
| **Avez-vous vu ma cravate? — Oui,** la *voilà* sur la chaise. | *Have you seen my tie? — Yes, there it is on the chair.* |
| *Il y a* une cravate sur la chaise. | *There is a tie on the chair.* |

**Il y a,** *ago* is used in expressions of time.

| | |
|---|---|
| **Je suis arrivé de New-York** *il y a* **huit jours.** | *I arrived from New York a week ago.* |

**106. Uses of** *falloir.*

*A.* The impersonal verb **falloir** translates the idea of the English *must.* It is followed by the subjunctive.

| | |
|---|---|
| *Il faut* que vous *alliez* voir ce film. | *You must go to see that picture.* |
| *Il a fallu* que je lui *écrive* cette lettre. | *I had to write him this letter.* |
| *Il faudra* que nous *partions* tout de suite après le concert. | *We will have to go away immediately after the concert.* |

*B.* The subjunctive construction may be replaced by **il me (te, lui, nous, vous, leur) faut** + infinitive. In this case, the pronoun subject of the dependent clause becomes the indirect object of **falloir.** This is not as frequently used as the subjunctive construction.

*Il me faut partir* } aujourd'hui,    *I must leave today, but my father*
*Il faut que je parte* }               *hasn't sent me any money yet.*
mais mon père ne m'a pas encore envoyé d'argent.

*C.* **Falloir** is followed by the infinitive to make a general statement with an impersonal subject.

| | |
|---|---|
| *Il faut faire attention* aux petits détails. | *One must pay attention to the little details.* |
| *Il faut boire* six verres d'eau par jour. | *One must drink six glasses of water a day.* |

*D.* **Il ne faut pas** and **il n'est pas nécessaire** are not synonymous. **Il ne faut pas** means *one mustn't;* **il n'est pas nécessaire** means *it is not necessary to, one doesn't have to.*

| | |
|---|---|
| *Il ne faut pas* nager après avoir mangé. | *You mustn't go swimming after eating.* |
| *Il n'est pas nécessaire* de lire tous ces livres. | *You don't have to read all these books.* |

*E.* **Falloir** is used with an indirect object to express need.

| | |
|---|---|
| *Il me faut* cent dollars tout de suite. | *I need a hundred dollars at once.* |
| *Il lui faudra* trois jours pour venir de Californie. | *He will need (take) three days to come from California.* |

**107. Uses of** *devoir.*

**Devoir** has several idiomatic meanings in addition to its regular meaning, *to owe.* The idiomatic tense uses may be grouped under four main heads, although it should be remembered that any attempt to reduce idiom to a system can be at best an approximation:

|  | Futurity *to be to* | Probability *must* | Unavoidable obligation *must* | Unfulfilled obligation *ought* |
|---|---|---|---|---|
| **Present** | 1) Present indicative or Future | 3) Present indicative | 5) Present indicative or Future | 7) Conditional |
| **Past** | 2) Imperfect indicative | 4) Past indefinite | 6) Past indefinite | 8) Past conditional |

EXAMPLES:

FUTURITY:

1) **Il *doit* partir ce soir.** *He is to leave this evening.*
*He is supposed (scheduled, expected) to leave this evening.*

**Il *devra* partir ce soir.** *He will be leaving this evening.*

2) **Il *devait* partir ce soir.** *He was to leave this evening.*
*He was supposed (scheduled, expected) to leave this evening.*

PROBABILITY:

3) **Il *doit* partir ce soir.** *He must be leaving this evening.*

4) **Il *a dû* partir ce soir.** *He must have been leaving this evening.*
*He must have left this evening.*

UNAVOIDABLE OBLIGATION:

5) **Il *doit* partir ce soir.** *He must leave this evening.*
*He has to leave this evening.*
*He is obliged to leave this evening.*
*It is necessary for him to leave this evening.*

**Il *devra* partir ce soir.** *He will have to leave this evening.*

6) Il *a dû* partir ce soir.

He had to leave this evening.
He was obliged to leave this evening.
It was necessary for him to leave this
evening.

UNFULFILLED OBLIGATION:

7) Il *devrait* partir ce soir.

He ought to leave this evening.
He should leave this evening.

8) Il *aurait dû* partir ce soir.

He ought to have left this evening.
He should have left this evening.

The problem can be approached from the opposite point of view: the various ways in which the idiomatic tense uses in French may be translated into English.

PRESENT INDICATIVE:

Il *doit* partir ce soir.

He is to leave this evening.
He is supposed (*scheduled, expected*)
to leave this evening.
He must be leaving this evening.
He must leave this evening.
He has to leave this evening.
He is obliged to leave this evening.
It is necessary for him to leave this
evening.

FUTURE:

Il *devra* partir ce soir.

He will be leaving this evening.
He will have to leave this evening.
It will be necessary for him to leave
this evening.

IMPERFECT:

Il *devait* partir ce soir.

He was to leave this evening.
He was supposed (*scheduled, expected*) to leave this evening.

PAST INDEFINITE:

Il *a dû* partir ce soir.

He must have been leaving this
evening.
He must have left this evening.
He had to leave this evening.
He was obliged to leave this evening.
It was necessary for him to leave this
evening.

CONDITIONAL:

Il *devrait* partir ce soir.                *He ought to leave this evening.*
                                            *He should leave this evening.*

PAST CONDITIONAL:

Il *aurait dû* partir ce soir.              *He ought to have left this evening.*
                                            *He should have left this evening.*

OBSERVATIONS:

1) The English word *must* is used to express both probability and obligation. Both these ideas are expressed in French by the present and past indefinite of **devoir**. Therefore, in translating from French to English, it may be necessary to ascertain from the context the more reasonable interpretation.

2) The past definite may, as usual, replace the past indefinite under the conditions already laid down (§ **79**) for the use of these two tenses.

3) Since *must* and *ought* have no past tense in English, the perfect infinitive (*have left*) must be added to express past time. **Devoir,** however, has all its tenses, and so, in examples 4), 6), and 8), past time is expressed by the appropriate tense of **devoir,** which is then followed by a present infinitive, **partir.**

**108.** *Devoir* and *falloir* Contrasted.

Both these verbs express obligation. Attempts have been made to distinguish between them on the basis that **devoir** indicates the inner origin of the obligation, while **falloir** suggests that the obligation is imposed from without. This distinction is not valid, as a study of cases will show, and it is obviously impossible to be dogmatic about expressions that depend so frequently on the intention of the speaker. It is true, however, that when the idea of duty or unavoidable obligation is clearly present, **devoir** should be preferred to **falloir.** Otherwise, **falloir** can be used safely, for it may express many shades of obligation from very weak to very strong. **Devoir** frequently replaces **falloir** in the compound past tenses, just because **j'ai dû** and **j'avais dû,** etc. are easier to use than **il a fallu que je . . . ,** and **il avait fallu que je . . . ,** etc.

## PART II

### 109. Uses of *vouloir*.

*A.* In general, **vouloir** means *to want*. It is not synonymous with **désirer,** which is less demanding in tone and might be translated by *to wish.*

| | |
|---|---|
| Je *désire* vous voir un instant. | *I wish to see you for a moment.* |
| Je *veux* vous voir tout de suite. | *I want to see you at once.* |

**Vouloir bien** means *to be willing.*

| | |
|---|---|
| Je *veux bien* vous accompagner. | *I am willing to go with you.* |

*B.* The distinctions that were made in § 77 between the use of the imperfect and past indefinite are equally applicable to this verb. If the state of wanting is not translated into action, the imperfect is used; if the desire becomes an action even for an instant, or if a serious attempt is made to convert it into action, the past indefinite is used.

| | |
|---|---|
| Je *voulais* voir mon père hier soir, mais il était parti pour la campagne dans l'après-midi. | *I wanted to see my father last evening, but he had left for the country in the afternoon.* |
| J'ai *voulu* lire ce livre, mais le premier chapitre m'a rebuté. | *I wanted to read that book, but the first chapter discouraged me.* |

*C.* The conditional expresses a politer request than the present indicative.

| | |
|---|---|
| *Voudriez*-vous me donner encore un verre d'eau? | *Would you please give me another glass of water?* |
| Je *voudrais* lui parler ce soir. | *I should like to speak to him this evening.* |

*D.* For an explanation of the use of *will* and *would* to express volition rather than mere futurity or the result of a condition, and the use of *will* and *would* to express habitual past action, see § **66, 67,** in Chapter Eight.

### 110. Uses of *pouvoir*.

*A.* **Pouvoir** expresses both ability (*can, could*) and possibility (*may, might*).

| | |
|---|---|
| Je *peux* vous accompagner maintenant. | *I can go with you now.* |
| Faites attention! Vous *pourriez* laisser tomber cette tasse. | *Watch out! You might let that cup fall.* |

*B.* In this verb, too, the past indefinite expresses a possibility translated into action, while the imperfect indicates that the possibility did not become a reality (Cf. § 109 *B*).

| | |
|---|---|
| J'*ai pu* lire ces trois livres en huit jours. | *I succeeded in reading these three books in a week.* |
| Je *pouvais* louer cette maison, mais je ne l'ai pas fait. | *It was possible for me to rent that house, but I didn't do it.* |

*C.* Since *can* and *may* cannot be conjugated in the compound tenses in English, the perfect infinitive of the dependent verb must be added to make good this lack. **Pouvoir,** however, has all its tenses, and so it needs only a present infinitive to complete its meaning, whether a simple or compound tense is demanded.

| | |
|---|---|
| Il *aurait pu* le *faire*. | *He could **have done it**.* |

### 111. Uses of *savoir*.

*A.* Savoir means *to know* (*a fact*), *to know thoroughly*, *to know how*.

| | |
|---|---|
| Il le *sait* par cœur. | *He knows it by heart.* |
| Je *sais* ce qu'il vous a montré. | *I know what he showed you.* |
| Mon ami *sait* chanter. | *My friend knows how to sing.* |

*B.* Savoir and **pouvoir** should not be confused.

| | |
|---|---|
| Mon ami ne *sait* pas patiner. | *My friend cannot skate (because he doesn't know how).* |
| Mon ami ne *peut* pas patiner, parce qu'il s'est cassé la jambe. | *My friend cannot skate, because he has broken his leg.* |

*C.* It is easy to confuse **savoir** with **connaître,** which means *to be acquainted with, to have some knowledge of,* a person or a thing.

| | |
|---|---|
| Il *sait* l'anglais et le français, et il *connaît* l'allemand et l'italien. | *He knows English and French well, and he has some acquaintance with German and Italian.* |
| *Connaissez*-vous ce monsieur? — Oui, je le *connais*. — *Savez*-vous ce qu'il fait ici? — Non, je ne le *sais* pas. | *Do you know that gentleman? — Yes, I know him. — Do you know what he is doing here? — No, I don't.* |

Connaissez-vous Londres ?　　Do you know London ?

Savez-vous quelle est la population　Do you know what the population
de Londres ?　　　　　　of London is ?

**112. Uses of *laisser*, etc.**

Laisser means *to let*, in the sense of *to permit*. The only problem in the use of this verb is that of word order.

*A.* When the dependent infinitive has no object or complement of its own, only a conjunctive object pronoun or a negative may come between **laisser** and the dependent infinitive.

Il *laisse tomber* le poids.　　*He lets the weight fall.*

Il ne *laisse pas tomber* le poids.　*He does not let the weight fall.*

*Laissez-le tomber.*　　　*Let it fall.*

*B.* When the dependent infinitive has an object or complement of its own, the word order parallels the English.

*Laissez mon frère travailler* pour　*Let my brother work for you.*
vous.

Je *laisse mon frère lire* tous mes　*I let my brother read all my books.*
livres.

*C.* The verbs **voir, regarder, entendre, écouter,** and **sentir** are used in the same construction as **laisser.**

Il *a vu s'éteindre* la lampe.　　*He saw the lamp go out.*

J'*ai regardé mon ami descendre*　*I watched my friend come down the*
l'escalier.　　　　　　*stair.*

Il *entend miauler* un chat.　　*He hears a cat mewing.*

J'*écoute chanter* mon ami.　　*I listen to my friend sing.*

Je *sens sa main me toucher* le vi-　*I feel his hand touch my face.*
sage.

**113. Uses of *faire*.**

*A.* The construction of **faire** + a dependent infinitive is often called by the type name of " **faire faire.** " Use of this combination of verbs implies that one does not do something oneself, but rather, that one has it done. The dependent infinitive follows **faire** directly, except for the possible intervention of a conjunctive object pronoun or a negative. These two sentences illustrate the simplest " **faire faire** " constructions and show that the following infinitive **may be** translated by either an active or a passive in English:

| | |
|---|---|
| Je *fais chanter* mon ami. | *I have my friend sing.* |
| Je *fais chanter* la chanson. | *I have the song sung.* |

*B.* When the dependent infinitive has its own direct object, the actual performer of the action becomes the indirect object.

| | |
|---|---|
| Elle fait peindre *son portrait à un artiste* connu. | *She is having her portrait painted by a well-known artist.* *She is having a well-known artist paint her portrait.* |

If these two noun objects are replaced by pronouns, the object pronouns precede **faire** and there is no agreement of the past participle of **faire**. The pronoun objects are arranged, of course, in their normal order (§ 35).

| | |
|---|---|
| Elle *le lui* fait peindre. | *She is having him paint it.* |
| Il *la lui* fait bâtir. | *He is having him build it.* |

*C.* A sentence like: **Il fait lire le poème à l'élève,** has two meanings: 1) *He has the student read the poem;* 2) *He has the poem read to the student.* To avoid this ambiguity the preposition **par** is used before the noun representing the performer of the action.

| | |
|---|---|
| Il fait lire le poème *par* l'élève. | *He has the student read the poem.* |

*D.* A reflexive pronoun is often used with the " **faire faire** " construction.

| | |
|---|---|
| Elle *se* fait faire une robe. | *She is having a dress made for herself.* |
| Il ne *se* fait jamais raser. | *He never has himself shaved.* |

**114. Use of *n'importe qui* (*lequel, quoi, quel*).**

*A.* When *anyone, anything,* and *any* + noun are not modified by a clause, they are translated by **n'importe** + **qui, lequel, quoi,** or **quel.**

| | |
|---|---|
| *N'importe qui* peut faire cela. | *Anyone at all can do that.* |
| Donnez-le à *n'importe qui.* | *Give it to anyone at all.* |
| Lequel choisissez-vous ? — Donnez-moi *n'importe lequel.* | *Which one do you chose? — Give me any one.* |
| Donnez-moi *n'importe quoi.* | *Give me anything at all.* |
| Allez dans *n'importe quelle* ville, et vous verrez la même chose. | *Go to any town at all, and you'll see the same thing.* |

*B.* When these same words are modified by a clause, they are translated by the appropriate combination of **tous ceux (qui, que,** etc.) or **tout ce (qui, que,** etc.).

| | |
|---|---|
| Il faut que *tous ceux qui* veulent partir demandent la permission. | *Anyone who wants to leave must ask permission.* |
| Je veux que vous disiez *tout ce qui* vous plaira. | *I want you to say anything that you please.* |

# CHAPTER FOURTEEN

## VERBS: THE PRESENT PARTICIPLE. THE INFINITIVE. ADVERBS. USES OF *TOUT*

### PART I

**115. Use of the Present Participle.**

*A.* In English the present participle is used after many prepositions:

He passed his examinations *without studying.*
Come to see me *before leaving.*
*Instead of answering,* he remained silent.

In French, however, only one preposition, **en,** may be followed by the present participle. Also, the present participle is the only construction that may follow **en.** Participial phrases may express 1) time, 2) parallel action, 3) manner, 4) means, etc.

1) *En lisant ce livre,* j'ai trouvé un passage très intéressant.    *While reading that book, I found a very interesting passage.*

2) Il ronfle *en dormant.*    *He snores while he sleeps.*
*Tout en parlant,* il me regardait du coin de l'œil.    *All the time that he was talking, he was watching me out of the corner of his eye.*

NOTE: **Tout** emphasizes the fact that the two actions are parallel.

3) Il est parti *en chantant.*    *He left singing.*

4) *En travaillant bien,* vous réussirez.    *By working hard, you will succeed.*

*B.* When the present participle is preceded by **en,** it always refers to the subject of the sentence. This rule may be seen in operation in the previous examples. Thus: **Je l'ai vue *en sortant* de la maison,** means *I saw her as I was leaving the house. I saw her leaving the house* would be translated **Je l'ai vue *qui sortait* de la maison.**

C. Sometimes the present participle is not preceded by **en.** Although it is difficult to formulate a rule that will enable the student to decide when to omit **en,** the following suggestions may be helpful: The participle with **en** modifies a verb. Used without **en,** it modifies a noun or pronoun. In practice, this is often a matter of the speaker's choice, as in the following sentences:

| | |
|---|---|
| *Riant,* il nous raconta ce qui lui était arrivé. | *Laughing, he told us what had happened to him.* |
| *Tout en riant,* il nous raconta ce qui lui était arrivé. | *Laughing all the while, he told us what had happened to him.* |

NOTE: The form with **tout en** gives more emphasis to the parallelism of the two actions.

| | |
|---|---|
| *Voyant* son frère *en sortant* de la bibliothèque, Marie lui a donné ses livres à porter. | *Seeing her brother as she came out of the library, Mary gave him her books to carry.* |

NOTE: The participial phrase beginning with **voyant** modifies Marie; the phrase beginning with **en sortant** modifies the participle **voyant** and refers to the subject of the sentence, **Marie.**

D. 1) The last example illustrates the fact that, when the participle is used verbally, it is invariable. When it is a true adjective, however, it agrees with its noun.

| | |
|---|---|
| Une ville *charmante.* | *A charming city.* |
| Une femme *mourante.* | *A dying woman.* |

2) Some verbs have a special form of the present participle that is used adjectivally.

| ADJECTIVE | PARTICIPLE |
|---|---|
| convaincant, *convincing* | convainquant |
| fatigant, *fatiguing* | fatiguant |
| puissant, *powerful* | pouvant |
| savant, *learned* | sachant |

## 116. Use of the Infinitive after Prepositions other than *en.*

A. No matter what the form of the English, the infinitive must be used in French after all prepositions but **en.**

| | |
|---|---|
| *Au lieu de répondre,* il s'est tu. | *Instead of answering, he remained silent.* |
| Venez me voir *avant de partir.* | *Come to see me before leaving.* |

116

| | |
|---|---|
| *Sans étudier,* il a passé ses examens avec succès. | *Without studying, he passed his examinations.* |
| *Après avoir visité* New-York, je suis rentré chez moi. | *After visiting New York, I returned home.* |

NOTE: The perfect infinitive must be used after après.

**B.** 1) **Pour** is used: *a)* when it is desirable to stress purpose; *b)* when the dependent infinitive is widely separated from the main verb of the sentence.

| | |
|---|---|
| *a)* Il est venu me parler hier soir. | *He came to speak to me last evening.* |
| Il est venu *pour* me parler d'une question importante. | *He came for the purpose of speaking to me about an important matter.* |

NOTE: The emphasis in the second sentence is on the object of the visit.

| | |
|---|---|
| *b)* Il est venu, dès que je suis rentré, *pour* me parler d'une question importante. | *He came, as soon as I returned, to speak to me about an important matter.* |

2) **Pour** is also used after **assez** and **trop.**

| | |
|---|---|
| Il est *assez* grand *pour* pouvoir voyager seul. | *He is big enough to travel alone.* |
| Il était *trop* malade *pour* me voir. | *He was too sick to see me.* |

**C. Par** is used only after the verbs **commencer** and **finir,** to translate the ideas of *beginning* or *ending by doing something.* These must not be confused with **commencer *à* faire** quelque chose, *to begin to do something,* and **finir *de* faire** quelque chose, *to finish doing something.*

| | |
|---|---|
| Il *a commencé par* nous lire la lettre. | *He began by reading us the letter.* |
| Il *a commencé à* lire la lettre. | *He began to read the letter.* |
| Il *a fini par* tout avouer. | *Finally, he confessed everything.* |
| Il *a fini de* travailler. | *He has finished working.* |

**D.** The use of **afin de, avant de, pour,** and **sans** with the infinitive instead of **afin que, avant que, pour que, sans que** with the subjunctive, when the subjects of the main verb and the dependent verb are identical, was discussed in § 92.

## 117. The Infinitive dependent upon a Verb.

**A.** Some verbs control a dependent infinitive directly without a preposition, others by the preposition **à,** still others by **de.** It is impossible to give rules that will aid in remembering how a given verb controls its dependent infinitive; such knowledge comes through practice. Fairly complete reference lists have been printed as Appendix III. Here it may be useful to condense those lists so as to include only the commonest verbs in each category.

1) Verbs that control a following infinitive directly without a preposition:

aimer mieux, *to prefer*
aller, *to go*
compter, *to expect*
courir, *to run*
croire, *to believe*
désirer, *to wish, to desire*
entendre, *to hear, to intend*
envoyer, *to send*
espérer, *to hope*
faire, *to make, to cause*
falloir, *must, to have to*
laisser, *to let, to allow*

oser, *to dare*
penser, *to think*
pouvoir, *to be able to*
préférer, *to prefer*
regarder, *to watch, to look at*
savoir, *to know how to, to be able*
sembler, *to seem, to appear*
valoir mieux, *to be better*
venir, *to come*
voir, *to see*
vouloir, *to want, to wish*

2) Verbs that control a following infinitive by à:

aider, *to help*
aimer, *to like*
amuser (s'), *to have a good time*
apprendre, *to learn, to teach*
attendre (s'), *to expect*
avoir, *to have*
chercher, *to seek*
commencer, *to begin*
consentir, *to consent*

continuer, *to continue*
décider (se), *to resolve*
enseigner, *to teach*
forcer, *to force*
inviter, *to invite*
mettre (se), *to begin*
obliger, *to oblige, to force*
réussir, *to succeed*
tenir, *to be anxious*

3) Verbs that control a following infinitive by de:

cesser, *to cease*
commencer, *to begin*
craindre, *to fear*
décider, *to decide*
défendre, *to prohibit*
demander, *to ask*
dépêcher (se), *to hurry*
dire, *to say*
empêcher, *to prevent*
essayer, *to try*

éviter, *to avoid*
finir, *to finish*
forcer, *to force*
manquer, *to fail*
offrir, *to offer*
ordonner, *to order*
oublier, *to forget*
permettre, *to permit*
persuader, *to persuade*
prendre garde, *to take care*

| | |
|---|---|
| promettre, *to promise* | remercier, *to thank* |
| refuser, *to refuse* | souvenir (se), *to remember* |
| regretter, *to regret* | tâcher, *to try* |

*B.* Some verbs, e.g., **commencer,** may govern the following infinitive by either **à** or **de.** It is suggested that the most usual method of control be learned to avoid confusion, although both may be met in reading.

*C.* The meaning of some verbs changes as the preposition changes. **Venir** is a good example.

| | |
|---|---|
| *Venez* me *voir.* | *Come to see me.* |
| Si vous *venez à* le *voir,* dites-lui bonjour de ma part. | *If you happen to see him, tell him hello for me.* |
| Je *viens de finir* mon travail. | *I have just finished my work.* |

**118. The Infinitive dependent upon a Noun or Adjective.**

*A.* The dependent infinitive as complement of an adjective or noun is usually preceded by **de.**

| | |
|---|---|
| Je suis *content de* vous *voir.* | *I am glad to see you.* |
| Il est *obligé de partir.* | *He is obliged to leave.* |
| Il est *digne d'être* récompensé. | *He is worthy of being rewarded.* |
| Il a l'*intention de partir.* | *He intends to leave.* |
| J'ai *envie de* le *voir.* | *I want to see him.* |

*B.* **Prêt,** exceptionally, is followed by **à.**

| | |
|---|---|
| Je suis *prêt à* vous *suivre.* | *I am ready to follow you.* |

*C.* In another connection (§ **21** *D*), sentences of the following types have been studied: **Il est facile de faire cela,** which follows the rule just given, and **C'est facile à faire,** which does not. Other constructions of the second type are common.

| | |
|---|---|
| J'ai quelque chose *à manger.* | *I have something to eat.* |
| C'est bon *à manger.* | *This is good to eat.* |
| J'ai du travail *à faire.* | *I have work to do.* |
| Il a une maison *à vendre.* | *He has a house to sell.* |

The rule is this: When the infinitive dependent on a noun or adjective may be made passive without violating English syntax or sense, it is preceded in French by **à.**

Le français est difficile *à apprendre.* *French is hard to learn.*

NOTE: The passive of the infinitive, *to be learned,* may be stilted, unidiomatic English, but from the standpoint of syntax and sense, it is acceptable. Hence, the infinitive preceded by à.

| | |
|---|---|
| Il est difficile *d'apprendre* le français. | *It is hard to learn French.* |

NOTE: The passive of the infinitive, *(hard) to be learned (French)*, makes no sense. Hence, the infinitive preceded by **de**.

## PART II

### 119. Simple Adverbs.

An adverb is a word that modifies a verb, an adjective, or another adverb. There are many simple adverbs in French, i.e., those that are not derived from corresponding adjectives. Such are:

aujourd'hui, *today*

déjà, *already*

derrière, *behind*

ici, *here*

moins, *less*

quand ?, *when ?*

surtout, *especially*

etc.

### 120. Adjectives used as Adverbs.

As noted in § **27** *C,* some adjectives may be used adverbially. When thus used, they are invariable.

| | |
|---|---|
| Parlez *bas.* | *Speak softly.* |
| Les roses sentent *bon.* | *Roses smell sweet.* |
| Les fleurs coûtent *cher.* | *Flowers are expensive.* |
| Elle l'arrête *court.* | *She stops him short.* |
| Elles parlent trop *haut.* | *They speak too loud.* |
| Ils marchent très *vite.* | *They walk very fast.* |

### 121. Formation of Adverbs from Adjectives.

Many French adverbs are formed by the addition of –**ment** to an adjective.

*A.* Most adjectives becomes adverbs through the addition of –ment to the feminine singular.

| MASCULINE | FEMININE | ADVERB |
|---|---|---|
| actif | active | activement, *actively* |
| cruel | cruelle | cruellement, *cruelly* |
| heureux | heureuse | heureusement, *happily* |
| mou | molle | mollement, *softly* |
| léger | légère | légèrement, *lightly* |
| facile | facile | facilement, *easily* |

**B.** Some common adjectives change the –e of the feminine to –é– before –**ment** is added.

| MASCULINE | FEMININE | ADVERB |
|---|---|---|
| commun | commune | communément, *commonly* |
| précis | précise | précisément, *precisely* |
| profond | profonde | profondément, *deeply* |

**C.** A few adjectives ending in –e change –e to –é– before –**ment** is added.

| MASCULINE AND FEMININE | ADVERB |
|---|---|
| aveugle | aveuglément, *blindly* |
| énorme | énormément, *enormously* |
| uniforme | uniformément, *uniformly* |
| | etc. |

**D.** Adjectives ending in a vowel, other than –e, form adverbs by adding –**ment** directly to the masculine singular form.

| ADJECTIVE | ADVERB | ADJECTIVE | ADVERB |
|---|---|---|---|
| poli | poliment, *politely* | infini | infiniment, *infinitely* |
| absolu | absolument, *absolutely* | vrai | vraiment, *truly* |
| décidé | décidément, *decidedly* | | |

**E.** Adjectives ending in –ant and –ent (except **lent, lentement,** *slowly*) change the final –nt to –m– and add –**ment**.

| ADJECTIVE | ADVERB | ADJECTIVE | ADVERB |
|---|---|---|---|
| constant | constamment, *constantly* | récent | récemment, *recently* |
| élégant | élégamment, *elegantly* | évident | évidemment, *evidently* |

### 122. Comparison of Adverbs.

**A.** Adverbs are compared like adjectives by the use of **plus, moins,** or **aussi** to form the comparative, and by the use of **le plus** or **le moins** to form the superlative. **Le** in the superlative is invariable. *Than, as* are translated by **que**.

POSITIVE:

Il parle *poliment.* — He speaks politely.

COMPARATIVE:

Il parle *plus (moins) poliment que* **vous.** — He speaks more (less) politely than you.

Il parle *aussi poliment que* **vous.** — He speaks as politely as you.

SUPERLATIVE:

| | |
|---|---|
| Il parle *le plus* (*le moins*) *poliment* de vous tous. | *He speaks the most (the least) politely of all of you.* |

*B.* Irregularly compared adverbs:

| POSITIVE | COMPARATIVE | SUPERLATIVE |
|---|---|---|
| bien, *well* | mieux, *better* | le mieux, *best* |
| mal, *ill, badly* | pis ⎱ plus mal ⎰, *worse* | le pis ⎱ le plus mal ⎰, *worst* |
| beaucoup, *much* | plus, *more* | le plus, *most* |
| peu, *little* | moins, *less* | le moins, *least* |

1) Confusion may arise between the adjective, **bon**, and the adverb, **bien**, because the word *well* is used as both adjective (health) and adverb (manner) in English, and because both *good* and *well* have the same comparative, *better*, and the same superlative, *best*.

2) The distinctions made between **plus mauvais** and **pire** in § 28 *B* 1 apply generally to **plus mal** and **pis**.

### 123. Position of Adverbs.

*A.* When used with the simple tenses of verbs, the adverb comes immediately after the verb.

| | |
|---|---|
| Il *parle lentement*. | *He speaks slowly.* |
| Il me *donne souvent* de l'argent. | *He often gives me money.* |

*B.* When used with the compound tenses of verbs, most simple adverbs (§ **119**) follow the auxiliary, while adverbs formed from adjectives (§ **121**) stand after the past participle.

| | |
|---|---|
| Il m'*a souvent* vu. | *He has seen me often.* |
| Il l'*a bien* reçu. | *He received him well.* |
| Nous l'avons *vu récemment*. | *We saw him recently.* |
| Ce film m'a *touché profondément*. | *That picture touched me deeply.* |

*C.* A few adverbs of time and place (**hier, aujourd'hui, demain, tôt, tard, ici, là, ailleurs, partout**) never come between the auxiliary and the past participle.

| | |
|---|---|
| Je l'ai *cherché partout*. | *I looked for it everywhere.* |
| Nous l'avons *vu hier*. | *We saw him yesterday.* |
| Il est *rentré tard*. | *He came in late.* |

**D.** Many adverbs may stand at the beginning of a sentence or after the verb for emphasis.

| | |
|---|---|
| *Malheureusement* je ne l'ai pas vu. | *Unfortunately I didn't see him.* |
| Je l'ai vu *déjà*. | *I have already seen him.* |

**124. Uses of *tout*.**

   *A.* As an adjective.

| | |
|---|---|
| Il a passé *toute* la journée chez moi. | *He spent all day at my house.* |
| Je le vois *tous* les jours. | *I see him every day.* |
| *Tous* mes amis sont venus. | *All my friends came.* |
| *Toutes* les roses sont mortes. | *All the roses are dead.* |

   *B.* As an adverb **tout** is invariable, except when it precedes a feminine adjective that begins with a consonant. In this case, it agrees with the adjective in gender and number.

| | |
|---|---|
| Il était *tout étonné*. | *He was completely astonished.* |
| Elle était *tout étonnée* (*heureuse*). | *She was completely astonished (happy).* |
| BUT: Elle est *toute petite*. | *She is quite small.* |
|    Elle était *toute honteuse*. | *She was completely ashamed.* |

NOTE: The **h** of **honteuse** is aspirate, with the value of a consonant.

   *C.* As a pronoun.

| | |
|---|---|
| *Tout* est pour le mieux. | *Everything is for the best.* |
| J'ai *tout* vu. | *I saw everything.* |
| Il vous aime *tous*. | *He likes you all.* |
| *Tous* sont venus. <br> Ils sont *tous* venus. | *They all came.* |
| Vous l'avez promis à nous *tous*. | *You promised it to all of us.* |

PRONUNCIATION NOTE: The final –s of **tous** is pronounced when **tous** is a pronoun; it is silent when **tous** is an adjective.

# APPENDIX I

**CONJUGATION OF *AVOIR, ETRE, PARLER, FINIR, VENDRE*. SPELLING PECULIARITIES OF FIRST CONJUGATION VERBS. CONJUGATION OF A REFLEXIVE VERB: *SE LAVER*.**

# A. AVOIR, *to have*

| Present Infinitive **avoir** | Present Participle **ayant** | Past Participle **eu** | Present Indicative **j'ai** | Past Definite **j'eus** |
|---|---|---|---|---|

*Future*
j'aurai
tu auras
il (elle) aura
nous aurons
vous aurez
ils (elles) auront

*Present Indicative*
(*plural*)
nous avons
vous avez
ils (elles) ont

COMPOUND TENSES

*Present Indicative*
(*singular*)
j'ai
tu as
il (elle) a

*Past Definite*
j'eus
tu eus
il (elle) eut
nous eûmes
vous eûtes
ils (elles) eurent

*Conditional*
j'aurais
tu aurais
il (elle) aurait
nous aurions
vous auriez
ils (elles) auraient

*Imperfect Indicative*
j'avais
tu avais
il (elle) avait
nous avions
vous aviez
ils (elles) avaient

*Past Indefinite*
j'ai eu, etc.

*Pluperfect Indicative*
j'avais eu, etc.

*Imperative*
aie
ayons
ayez

*Imperfect Subjunctive*
j'eusse
tu eusses
il (elle) eût
nous eussions
vous eussiez
ils (elles) eussent

*Present Subjunctive*
j'aie
tu aies
il (elle) ait
nous ayons
vous ayez
ils (elles) aient

*Past Anterior*
j'eus eu, etc.

*Future Perfect*
j'aurai eu, etc.

*Past Conditional*
j'aurais eu, etc.

*Perfect Subjunctive*
j'aie eu, etc.

*Pluperfect Subjunctive*
j'eusse eu, etc.

## B. ETRE, to be

**Present Infinitive**
être

**Present Participle**
étant

**Past Participle**
été

**Past Definite**
je fus

**Present Indicative**
je suis

**Future**
je serai
tu seras
il (elle) sera
nous serons
vous serez
ils (elles) seront

**Present Indicative (plural)**
nous sommes
vous êtes
ils (elles) sont

**Present Indicative (singular)**
je suis
tu es
il (elle) est

**Past Definite**
je fus
tu fus
il (elle) fut
nous fûmes
vous fûtes
ils (elles) furent

**Conditional**
je serais
tu serais
il (elle) serait
nous serions
vous seriez
ils (elles) seraient

**Imperfect Indicative**
j'étais
tu étais
il (elle) était
nous étions
vous étiez
ils (elles) étaient

**Imperative**
sois
soyons
soyez

**Imperfect Subjunctive**
je fusse
tu fusses
il (elle) fût
nous fussions
vous fussiez
ils (elles) fussent

**Present Subjunctive**
je sois
tu sois
il (elle) soit
nous soyons
vous soyez
ils (elles) soient

### COMPOUND TENSES

**Past Indefinite**
j'ai été, etc.

**Pluperfect Indicative**
j'avais été, etc.

**Past Anterior**
j'eus été, etc.

**Future Perfect**
j'aurai été, etc.

**Past Conditional**
j'aurais été, etc.

**Perfect Subjunctive**
j'aie été, etc.

**Pluperfect Subjunctive**
j'eusse été, etc.

## C. PARLER, to speak

| Present Infinitive | Present Participle | Past Participle | Present Indicative | Past Definite |
|---|---|---|---|---|
| **parler** | **parlant** | **parlé** | **je parle** | **je parlai** |

*Present Indicative (singular)*
je parle
tu parles
il (elle) parle

*Present Indicative (plural)*
nous parlons
vous parlez
ils (elles) parlent

*Future*
je parlerai
tu parleras
il (elle) parlera
nous parlerons
vous parlerez
ils (elles) parleront

*Past Definite*
je parlai
tu parlas
il (elle) parla
nous parlâmes
vous parlâtes
ils (elles) parlèrent

*Imperfect Indicative*
je parlais
tu parlais
il (elle) parlait
nous parlions
vous parliez
ils (elles) parlaient

*Imperfect Subjunctive*
je parlasse
tu parlasses
il (elle) parlât
nous parlassions
vous parlassiez
ils (elles) parlassent

*Conditional*
je parlerais
tu parlerais
il (elle) parlerait
nous parlerions
vous parleriez
ils (elles) parleraient

*Present Subjunctive*
je parle
tu parles
il (elle) parle
nous parlions
vous parliez
ils (elles) parlent

*Imperative*
parle
parlons
parlez

COMPOUND TENSES

*Past Indefinite*
j'ai parlé, etc.

*Pluperfect Indicative*
j'avais parlé, etc.

*Past Anterior*
j'eus parlé, etc.

*Future Perfect*
j'aurai parlé, etc.

*Past Conditional*
j'aurais parlé, etc.

*Perfect Subjunctive*
j'aie parlé, etc.

*Pluperfect Subjunctive*
j'eusse parlé, etc.

129

## D. FINIR, to finish

| Present Infinitive | Present Participle | Past Participle | Present Indicative | Past Definite |
|---|---|---|---|---|
| **finir** | **finissant** | **fini** | **je finis** | **je finis** |

**Future**
je finirai
tu finiras
il (elle) finira
nous finirons
vous finirez
ils (elles) finiront

**Conditional**
je finirais
tu finirais
il (elle) finirait
nous finirions
vous finiriez
ils (elles) finiraient

**Present Indicative**
*(plural)*
nous finissons
vous finissez
ils (elles) finissent

**Imperfect Indicative**
je finissais
tu finissais
il (elle) finissait
nous finissions
vous finissiez
ils (elles) finissaient

**Present Subjunctive**
je finisse
tu finisses
il (elle) finisse
nous finissions
vous finissiez
ils (elles) finissent

COMPOUND TENSES

**Past Indefinite**
j'ai fini, etc.

**Pluperfect Indicative**
j'avais fini, etc.

**Past Anterior**
j'eus fini, etc.

**Future Perfect**
j'aurai fini, etc.

**Past Conditional**
j'aurais fini, etc.

**Perfect Subjunctive**
j'aie fini, etc.

**Pluperfect Subjunctive**
j'eusse fini, etc.

**Present Indicative**
*(singular)*
je finis
tu finis
il (elle) finit

**Imperative**
finis
finissons
finissez

**Past Definite**
je finis
tu finis
il (elle) finit
nous finîmes
vous finîtes
ils (elles) finirent

**Imperfect Subjunctive**
je finisse
tu finisses
il (elle) finît
nous finissions
vous finissiez
ils (elles) finissent

## E. VENDRE, to sell

| Present Infinitive vendre | Present Participle vendant | Present Indicative je vends | Past Participle vendu | Present Indicative je vends | Past Definite je vendis |
|---|---|---|---|---|---|

*Future*
je vendrai
tu vendras
il (elle) vendra
nous vendrons
vous vendrez
ils (elles) vendront

*Present Indicative (plural)*
nous vendons
vous vendez
ils (elles) vendent

*Present Indicative (singular)*
je vends
tu vends
il (elle) vend*

COMPOUND TENSES

*Present Indicative (singular)*
je vends
tu vends
il (elle) vend*

*Past Definite*
je vendis
tu vendis
il (elle) vendit
nous vendîmes
vous vendîtes
ils (elles) vendirent

*Imperfect Indicative*
je vendais
tu vendais
il (elle) vendait
nous vendions
vous vendiez
ils (elles) vendaient

*Past Indefinite*
j'ai vendu, etc.

*Pluperfect Indicative*
j'avais vendu, etc.

*Imperative*
vends
vendons
vendez

*Imperfect Subjunctive*
je vendisse
tu vendisses
il (elle) vendît
nous vendissions
vous vendissiez
ils (elles) vendissent

*Conditional*
je vendrais
tu vendrais
il (elle) vendrait
nous vendrions
vous vendriez
ils (elles) vendraient

*Present Subjunctive*
je vende
tu vendes
il (elle) vende
nous vendions
vous vendiez
ils (elles) vendent

*Past Anterior*
j'eus vendu, etc.

*Future Perfect*
j'aurai vendu, etc.

*Past Conditional*
j'aurais vendu, etc.

*Perfect Subjunctive*
j'aie vendu, etc.

*Pluperfect Subjunctive*
j'eusse vendu, etc.

* When the final stem consonant is not **c**, **t**, or **d**, the ending –t is added to the third person singular of the present indicative: **il rompt.**

131

## F. Spelling Peculiarities of First Conjugation Verbs.

In certain verbs of the first conjugation, changes in spelling occur for purely phonetic reasons. Such verbs fall into four classes: 1) verbs ending in –cer; 2) verbs ending in –ger; 3) verbs ending in –yer; 4) verbs with the stem vowel **mute e** or **é.**

1) In order to preserve the soft (s) sound of **c** throughout the conjugation of verbs ending in **–cer,** it is necessary to place a cedilla under the **c** whenever it occurs before an **a** or an **o** of an ending.

| | | |
|---|---|---|
| INFINITIVE: | avancer | |
| PRESENT PARTICIPLE: | avançant | |
| PRESENT INDICATIVE: | nous avançons (BUT: vous avancez) | |
| IMPERFECT INDICATIVE: | j'avançais | il avançait |
| | tu avançais | ils avançaient |
| PAST DEFINITE: | j'avançai | nous avançâmes |
| | tu avanças | vous avançâtes |
| | il avança (BUT: ils avancèrent) | |

IMPERFECT SUBJUNCTIVE: j'avançasse, etc.

2) Similarly, the soft sound of **g** is preserved throughout the conjugation of verbs ending in **–ger** by inserting a **mute e** between the **g** of the stem and an **a** or an **o** of the ending.

| | | |
|---|---|---|
| INFINITIVE: | manger | |
| PRESENT PARTICIPLE: | mangeant | |
| PRESENT INDICATIVE: | nous mangeons | |
| IMPERFECT INDICATIVE: | je mangeais | (BUT: nous mangions) |
| | tu mangeais | (BUT: vous mangiez) |
| | il mangeait | ils mangeaient |
| PAST DEFINITE: | je mangeai | nous mangeâmes |
| | tu mangeas | vous mangeâtes |
| | il mangea | (BUT: ils mangèrent) |

IMPERFECT SUBJUNCTIVE: je mangeasse, etc.

3) Verbs ending in –oyer and –uyer change y to i whenever **y** comes before a **mute e,** but not elsewhere. Verbs ending in –ayer or –eyer may retain the **y** throughout, although in these cases, too, the change may be made.

| | |
|---|---|
| INFINITIVE: | nettoyer, essuyer, payer |
| PRESENT INDICATIVE: | je nettoie, etc. |
| | j'essuie, etc. |
| | je paie or je paye, etc. |
| FUTURE: | je nettoierai, etc. |
| | j'essuierai, etc. |
| | je paierai or je payerai, etc. |
| CONDITIONAL: | je nettoierais, etc. |
| | j'essuierais, etc. |
| | je paierais or je payerais, etc. |

4) The problem of verbs whose stem vowel is **mute e** or **é** is more complicated.

*a*) When the stem vowel is **mute e,** this vowel must be changed to **è** whenever the following syllable also contains a **mute e.**

INFINITIVE: mener

PRESENT INDICATIVE:

| je mène | (following syllable con-tains **mute e**) | nous menons | (following syllable does not contain **mute e**) |
|---|---|---|---|
| tu mènes | | vous menez | |
| il mène | | ils mènent | (following syllable con-tains **mute e**) |

PRESENT SUBJUNCTIVE:

| je mène | nous menions |
|---|---|
| tu mènes | vous meniez |
| il mène | ils mènent |

In the future and conditional, the syllable after the stem vowel is always mute; hence, the stem vowel is **è** throughout these tenses.

je mènerai, je mènerais, etc.

*b*) When the stem vowel is **é,** this vowel is changed to **è** only in the present indicative and present subjunctive whenever the following syllable contains a **mute e.**

INFINITIVE: céder

PRESENT INDICATIVE:

| je cède | nous cédons |
|---|---|
| tu cèdes | vous cédez |
| il cède | ils cèdent |

PRESENT SUBJUNCTIVE:

| | |
|---|---|
| je cède | nous cédions |
| tu cèdes | vous cédiez |
| il cède | ils cèdent |

In the future and conditional, however, the **é** remains.

je céderai, je céderais, etc.

Verbs like **créer,** in which the stem vowel **é** is followed by another vowel, are regular.

*c)* Most verbs ending in **–eler** and **–eter** show the change from **mute e** by doubling the consonant rather than by adding the grave accent.

INFINITIVE: appeler (jeter)

PRESENT INDICATIVE:

| | |
|---|---|
| j'appelle (jette) | nous appelons (jetons) |
| tu appelles (jettes) | vous appelez (jetez) |
| il appelle (jette) | ils appellent (jettent) |

PRESENT SUBJUNCTIVE:

| | |
|---|---|
| j'appelle (jette) | nous appelions (jetions) |
| tu appelles (jettes) | vous appeliez (jetiez) |
| il appelle (jette) | ils appellent (jettent) |

FUTURE:

| | |
|---|---|
| j'appellerai (jetterai) | nous appellerons (jetterons) |
| tu appelleras (jetteras) | vous appellerez (jetterez) |
| il appellera (jettera) | ils appelleront (jetteront) |

CONDITIONAL:

j'appellerais (jetterais), etc.

NOTE: A few common verbs take the grave accent just like **mener**: **acheter,** *to buy;* **geler,** *to freeze;* **modeler,** *to model;* **peler,** *to peel;* etc.

## G. Conjugation of a Reflexive Verb.

INFINITIVE: **se laver**

PRESENT PARTICIPLE: **se lavant**

PAST PARTICIPLE: **lavé**

PRESENT INDICATIVE AFFIRMATIVE:

| | |
|---|---|
| **je me lave** | nous nous lavons |
| tu te laves | vous vous lavez |
| il (elle) se lave | ils (elles) se lavent |

# APPENDIX I

PRESENT INDICATIVE INTERROGATIVE:

| | |
|---|---|
| est-ce que je me lave ? | nous lavons-nous ? |
| te laves-tu ? | vous lavez-vous ? |
| se lave-t-il (-elle) ? | se lavent-ils (-elles) ? |

PRESENT INDICATIVE NEGATIVE:

| | |
|---|---|
| je ne me lave pas | nous ne nous lavons pas |
| tu ne te laves pas | vous ne vous lavez pas |
| il (elle) ne se lave pas | ils (elles) ne se lavent pas |

IMPERATIVE:

lave-toi
lavons-nous
lavez-vous

FUTURE: je me laverai, etc.

CONDITIONAL: je me laverais, etc.

IMPERFECT: je me lavais, etc.

PAST DEFINITE: **je me lavai,** etc.

PAST INDEFINITE:

| | |
|---|---|
| je me suis lavé(e) | nous nous sommes lavé(e)s |
| tu t'es lavé(e) | vous vous êtes lavé(e)s |
| il (elle) s'est lavé(e) | ils (elles) se sont lavé(e)s |

PLUPERFECT: je m'étais lavé(e), etc.

PAST ANTERIOR: je me fus lavé(e), etc.

FUTURE PERFECT: je me serai lavé(e), etc.

PAST CONDITIONAL: je me serais lavé(e), etc.

PRESENT SUBJUNCTIVE: je me lave, etc.

IMPERFECT SUBJUNCTIVE: je me lavasse, etc.

PERFECT SUBJUNCTIVE: je me sois lavé(e), etc.

PLUPERFECT SUBJUNCTIVE: je me fusse lavé(e), etc.

# APPENDIX II

## CONJUGATION OF IRREGULAR VERBS

**1. Acquérir,** *to acquire.*

1. *Inf.* **acquérir;** *Fut.* acquerrai, etc.; *Cond.* acquerrais, etc.
2. *Pres. part.* **acquérant;** *Imp. ind.* acquérais, etc.; *Pres. subj.* acquière, acquières, acquière, acquérions, acquériez, acquièrent.
3. *Past part.* **acquis;** *Past indef.* ai acquis, etc.
4. *Pres. ind.* **acquiers,** acquiers, acquiert, acquérons, acquérez, acquièrent; *Impv.* acquiers, acquérons, acquérez.
5. *Past def.* **acquis,** acquis, acquit, acquîmes, acquîtes, acquirent; *Imp. subj.* acquisse, acquisses, acquît, etc.

Like **acquérir:** conquérir, *to conquer.*

**2. Aller,** *to go.*

1. *Inf.* **aller;** *Fut.* irai, etc.; *Cond.* irais, etc.
2. *Pres. part.* **allant;** *Imp. ind.* allais, etc.; *Pres. subj.* aille, ailles, aille, allions, alliez, aillent.
3. *Past part.* **allé;** *Past indef.* suis allé, etc.
4. *Pres. ind.* **vais,** vas, va, allons, allez, vont; *Impv.* va, allons, allez.
5. *Past def.* **allai,** allas, alla, allâmes, allâtes, allèrent; *Imp. subj.* allasse, allasses, allât, etc.

Like **aller:** s'en aller, *to go away.*

**3. Asseoir,** *to seat.*

1. *Inf.* **asseoir;** *Fut.* assiérai, *or* assoirai, etc.; *Cond.* assiérais *or* assoirais, etc.
2. *Pres. part.* **asseyant** or assoyant; *Imp. ind.* asseyais *or* assoyais, etc.; *Pres. subj.* asseye, asseyes, asseye, asseyions, asseyiez, asseyent *or* assoie, assoies, assoie, assoyions, assoyiez, assoient.
3. *Past part.* **assis;** *Past indef.* ai assis, etc.
4. *Pres. ind.* **assieds,** assieds, assied, asseyons, asseyez, asseyent *or* assois, assois, assoit, assoyons, assoyez, assoient; *Impv.* assieds, asseyons, asseyez *or* assois, assoyons, assoyez.
5. *Past def.* **assis,** assis, assit, assîmes, assîtes, assirent; *Imp. subj.* assisse, assisses, assît, etc.

Like **asseoir:** s'asseoir, *to sit down.*

136

# APPENDIX II

**4. Boire,** *to drink.*

1. *Inf.* **boire;** *Fut.* boirai, etc.; *Cond.* boirais, etc.
2. *Pres. part.* **buvant;** *Imp. ind.* buvais, etc.; *Pres. subj.* boive, boives, boive, buvions, buviez, boivent.
3. *Past part.* **bu;** *Past indef.* ai bu, etc.
4. *Pres. ind.* **bois,** bois, boit, buvons, buvez, boivent; *Impv.* bois, buvons, buvez.
5. *Past def.* **bus,** bus, but, bûmes, bûtes, burent; *Imp. subj.* busse, busses, bût, etc.

**5. Conclure,** *to conclude.*

1. *Inf.* **conclure;** *Fut.* conclurai, etc.; *Cond.* conclurais, etc.
2. *Pres. part.* **concluant;** *Imp. ind.* concluais, etc.; *Pres. subj.* conclue, conclues, conclue, concluions, concluiez, concluent.
3. *Past part.* **conclu;** *Past indef.* ai conclu, etc.
4. *Pres. ind.* **conclus,** conclus, conclut, concluons, concluez, concluent; *Impv.* conclus, concluons, concluez.
5. *Past def.* **conclus,** conclus, conclut, conclûmes, conclûtes, conclurent; *Imp. subj.* conclusse, conclusses, conclût, etc.

Like **conclure:** exclure, *to exclude.*

**6. Conduire,** *to conduct, to lead, to take.*

1. *Inf.* **conduire;** *Fut.* conduirai, etc.; *Cond.* conduirais, etc.
2. *Pres. part.* **conduisant;** *Imp. ind.* conduisais, etc.; *Pres. subj.* conduise, conduises, conduise, conduisions, conduisiez, conduisent.
3. *Past part.* **conduit;** *Past indef.* ai conduit, etc.
4. *Pres. ind.* **conduis,** conduis, conduit, conduisons, conduisez, conduisent; *Impv.* conduis, conduisons, conduisez.
5. *Past def.* **conduisis,** conduisis, conduisit, conduisîmes, conduisîtes, conduisirent; *Imp. subj.* conduisisse, conduisisses, conduisît, etc.

Like **conduire:** construire, *to build;* détruire, *to destroy;* instruire, *to instruct;* produire, *to produce;* réduire, *to reduce;* traduire, *to translate;* etc.

**7. Connaître,** *to know,* etc.

1. *Inf.* **connaître;** *Fut.* connaîtrai, etc.; *Cond.* connaîtrais, etc.
2. *Pres. part.* **connaissant;** *Imp. ind.* connaissais, etc.; *Pres. subj.* connaisse, connaisses, connaisse, connaissions, connaissiez, connaissent.
3. *Past part.* **connu;** *Past indef.* ai connu, etc.
4. *Pres. ind.* **connais,** connais, connaît, connaissons, connaissez, connaissent; *Impv.* connais, connaissons, connaissez.
5. *Past def.* **connus,** connus, connut, connûmes, connûtes, connurent; *Imp. subj.* connusse, connusses, connût, etc.

Like **connaître:** reconnaître, *to recognize;* paraître, *to seem;* apparaître, *to appear;* disparaître, *to disappear;* reparaître, *to reappear.*

**8. Coudre,** *to sew.*

1. *Inf.* **coudre;** *Fut.* coudrai, etc.; *Cond.* coudrais, etc.

2. *Pres. part.* **cousant;** *Imp. ind.* cousais, etc.; *Pres. subj.* couse, couses, couse, cousions, cousiez, cousent.

3. *Past part.* **cousu;** *Past indef.* ai cousu, etc.

4. *Pres. ind.* **couds,** couds, coud, cousons, cousez, cousent; *Impv.* couds, cousons, cousez.

5. *Past def.* **cousis,** cousis, cousit, cousîmes, cousîtes, cousirent; *Imp. subj.* cousisse, cousisses, cousît, etc.

Like **coudre:** découdre, *to rip, to unsew;* recoudre, *to sew up again.*

**9. Courir,** *to run.*

1. *Inf.* **courir;** *Fut.* courrai, etc.; *Cond.* courrais, etc.

2. *Pres. part.* **courant;** *Imp. ind.* courais, etc.; *Pres. subj.* coure, coures, coure, courions, couriez, courent.

3. *Past part.* **couru;** *Past indef.* ai couru, etc.

4. *Pres. ind.* **cours,** cours, court, courons, courez, courent; *Impv.* cours, courons, courez.

5. *Past def.* **courus,** courus, courut, courûmes, courûtes, coururent; *Imp. subj.* courusse, courusses, courût, etc.

Like **courir:** accourir, *to run up, to hasten;* parcourir, *to travel over, to look through.*

**10. Craindre,** *to fear.*

1. *Inf.* **craindre;** *Fut.* craindrai, etc.; *Cond.* craindrais, etc.

2. *Pres. part.* **craignant;** *Imp. ind.* craignais, etc.; *Pres. subj.* craigne, craignes, craigne, craignions, craigniez, craignent.

3. *Past part.* **craint;** *Past indef.* ai craint, etc.

4. *Pres. ind.* **crains,** crains, craint, craignons, craignez, craignent; *Impv.* crains, craignons, craignez.

5. *Past def.* **craignis,** craignis, craignit, craignîmes, craignîtes, craignirent *Imp. subj.* craignisse, craignisses, craignît, etc.

Like **craindre:** plaindre, *to pity;* se plaindre, *to complain;* éteindre, *to extinguish;* atteindre, *to reach;* peindre, *to paint;* rejoindre, *to catch up with* joindre, *to join.*

**11. Croire,** *to believe.*

1. *Inf.* **croire;** *Fut.* croirai, etc.; *Cond.* croirais, etc.

2. *Pres. part.* **croyant;** *Imp. ind.* croyais, etc.; *Pres. subj.* croie, croie croie, croyions, croyiez, croient.

3. *Past part.* **cru;** *Past indef.* ai cru, etc.

4. *Pres. ind.* **crois,** crois, croit, croyons, croyez, croient; *Impv.* croi croyons, croyez.

5. *Past def.* **crus,** crus, crut, crûmes, crûtes, crurent; *Imp. subj.* cruss crusses, crût, etc.

# APPENDIX II

**12.** Croître, *to grow.*

1. *Inf.* **croître**; *Fut.* croîtrai, etc.; *Cond.* croîtrais, etc.

2. *Pres. part.* **croissant**; *Imp. ind.* croissais, etc.; *Pres. subj.* croisse, croisses, croisse, croissions, croissiez, croissent.

3. *Past part.* **crû**; *Past indef.* ai crû, etc.

4. *Pres. ind.* **croîs**, croîs, croît, croissons, croissez, croissent; *Impv.* croîs, croissons, croissez.

5. *Past def.* **crûs**, crûs, crût, crûmes, crûtes, crûrent; *Imp. subj.* crusse, crusses, crût, etc.

NOTE: The circumflex accent distinguishes between the forms of **croître** and **croire** that would otherwise be identical.

**13.** Cueillir, *to gather, to pick.*

1. *Inf.* **cueillir**; *Fut.* cueillerai, etc.; *Cond.* cueillerais, etc.

2. *Pres. part.* **cueillant**; *Imp. ind.* cueillais, etc.; *Pres. subj.* cueille, cueilles, cueille, cueillions, cueilliez, cueillent.

3. *Past part.* **cueilli**; *Past indef.* ai cueilli, etc.

4. *Pres. ind.* **cueille,** cueilles, cueille, cueillons, cueillez, cueillent; *Impv.* cueille, cueillons, cueillez.

5. *Past def.* **cueillis**, cueillis, cueillit, cueillîmes, cueillîtes, cueillirent; *Imp. subj.* cueillisse, cueillisses, cueillît, etc.

Like **cueillir:** accueillir, *to welcome;* recueillir, *to gather, to collect;* tressaillir, *to start, to tremble.*

**14.** Devoir, *to owe, must,* etc.

1. *Inf.* **devoir**; *Fut.* devrai, etc.; *Cond.* devrais, etc.

2. *Pres. part.* **devant;** *Imp. ind.* devais, etc.; *Pres. subj.* doive, doives, doive, devions, deviez, doivent.

3. *Past part.* **dû** (*f.* due, *pl.* du(e)s); *Past indef.* ai dû, etc.

4. *Pres. ind.* **dois,** dois, doit, devons, devez, doivent.

5. *Past def.* **dus**, dus, dut, dûmes, dûtes, durent; *Imp. subj.* dusse, dusses, dût, etc.

**15.** Dire, *to say, to tell.*

1. *Inf.* **dire**; *Fut.* dirai, etc.; *Cond.* dirais, etc.

2. *Pres. part.* **disant**; *Imp. ind.* disais, etc.; *Pres. subj.* dise, dises, dise, disions, disiez, disent.

3. *Past part.* **dit**; *Past indef.* ai dit, etc.

4. *Pres. ind.* **dis**, dis, dit, disons, dites, disent; *Impv.* dis, disons, dites.

5. *Past def.* **dis**, dis, dit, dîmes, dîtes, dirent; *Imp. subj.* disse, disses, dît, etc.

Like **dire:** contredire,[1] *to contradict;* interdire,[1] *to forbid;* médire,[1] *to slander;* prédire,[1] *to predict;* redire, *to repeat.*

[1] Second plur. pres. indic. and impv.: contredisez, interdisez, etc.

**16. Dormir,** *to sleep.*

1. *Inf.* **dormir;** *Fut.* dormirai, etc.; *Cond.* dormirais, etc.

2. *Pres. part.* **dormant;** *Imp. ind.* dormais, etc.; *Pres. subj.* dorme, dormes, dorme, dormions, dormiez, dorment.

3. *Past part.* **dormi;** *Past indef.* ai dormi, etc.

4. *Pres. ind.* **dors,** dors, dort, dormons, dormez, dorment; *Impv.* dors, dormons, dormez.

5. *Past def.* **dormis,** dormis, dormit, dormîmes, dormîtes, dormirent; *Imp. subj.* dormisse, dormisses, dormît, etc.

Like **dormir:** endormir, *to put to sleep;* s'endormir, *to go to sleep;* se rendormir, *to go back to sleep;* se repentir, *to repent;* bouillir, *to boil* (*Pres. ind.* bous, bous, bout, bouillons, bouillez, bouillent); sentir, *to feel;* consentir, *to consent;* ressentir, *to resent, to feel;* servir, *to serve;* se servir de, *to make use of;* mentir, *to lie;* partir, *to leave* (*aux.* être); repartir, *to set out again* (*aux.* être), *to reply* (*aux.* avoir); sortir, *to go out* (*aux.* être).

**17. Écrire,** *to write.*

1. *Inf.* **écrire;** *Fut.* écrirai, etc.; *Cond.* écrirais, etc.

2. *Pres. part.* **écrivant;** *Imp. ind.* écrivais, etc.; *Pres. subj.* écrive, écrives, écrive, écrivions, écriviez, écrivent.

3. *Past part.* **écrit;** *Past indef.* ai écrit, etc.

4. *Pres. ind.* **écris,** écris, écrit, écrivons, écrivez, écrivent; *Impv.* écris, écrivons, écrivez.

5. *Past def.* **écrivis,** écrivis, écrivit, écrivîmes, écrivîtes, écrivirent; *Imp. subj.* écrivisse, écrivisses, écrivît, etc.

Like **écrire:** décrire, *to describe;* inscrire, *to inscribe;* prescrire, *to prescribe.*

**18. Envoyer,** *to send.*

1. *Inf.* **envoyer;** *Fut.* enverrai, etc.; *Cond.* enverrais, etc.

2. *Pres. part.* **envoyant;** *Imp. ind.* envoyais, envoyais, envoyait, envoyions, envoyiez, envoyaient; *Pres. subj.* envoie, envoies, envoie, envoyions, envoyiez, envoient.

3. *Past part.* **envoyé;** *Past indef.* ai envoyé, etc.

4. *Pres. ind.* **envoie,** envoies, envoie, envoyons, envoyez, envoient; *Impv.* envoie, envoyons, envoyez.

5. *Past def.* **envoyai,** envoyas, envoya, envoyâmes, envoyâtes, envoyèrent; *Imp. subj.* envoyasse, envoyasses, envoyât, etc.

Like **envoyer:** renvoyer, *to send away, to dismiss.*

**19. Faire,** *to do, to make.*

1. *Inf.* **faire;** *Fut.* ferai, etc.; *Cond.* ferais, etc.

2. *Pres. part.* **faisant;** *Imp. ind.* faisais, etc.; *Pres. subj.* fasse, fasses, fasse, fassions, fassiez, fassent.

3. *Past part.* **fait;** *Past indef.* ai fait, etc.

4. *Pres ind.* **fais,** fais, fait, faisons, faites, font; *Impv.* fais, faisons, faites.
5. *Past def.* **fis,** fis, fit, fîmes, fîtes, firent; *Imp. subj.* fisse, fisses, fît, etc.
Like **faire:** satisfaire, *to satisfy.*

**20. Falloir,** *must.*

1. *Inf.* **falloir;** *Fut.* il faudra; *Cond.* il faudrait.
2. *Imp. ind.* il fallait; *Pres. subj.* il faille.
3. *Past part.* **fallu;** *Past indef.* il a fallu.
4. *Pres. ind.* il **faut.**
5. *Past def.* il **fallut;** *Imp. subj.* il fallût.

**21. Fuir,** *to flee.*

1. *Inf.* **fuir;** *Fut.* fuirai, etc.; *Cond.* fuirais, etc.
2. *Pres. part.* **fuyant;** *Imp. ind.* fuyais, etc.; *Pres. subj.* fuie, fuies, fuie, fuyions, fuyiez, fuient.
3. *Past part.* **fui;** *Past indef.* ai fui, etc.
4. *Pres. ind.* **fuis,** fuis, fuit, fuyons, fuyez, fuient; *Impv.* fuis, fuyons, fuyez.
5. *Past def.* **fuis,** fuis, fuit, fuîmes, fuîtes, fuirent; *Imp. subj.* fuisse, fuisses, fuît, etc.
Like **fuir:** s'enfuir, *to flee, to escape.*

**22. Haïr,** *to hate.*

1. *Inf.* **haïr;** *Fut.* haïrai, etc.; *Cond.* haïrais, etc.
2. *Pres. part.* **haïssant;** *Imp. ind.* haïssais, etc.; *Pres. subj.* haïsse, haïsses, haïsse, haïssions, haïssiez, haïssent.
3. *Past part.* **haï;** *Past indef.* ai haï, etc.
4. *Pres. ind.* **hais,** hais, hait, haïssons, haïssez, haïssent; *Impv.* hais, haïssons, haïssez.
5. *Past def.* **haïs,** haïs, haït, haïmes, haïtes, haïrent; *Imp. subj.* haïsse, haïsses, haït, etc.

**23. Lire,** *to read.*

1. *Inf.* **lire;** *Fut.* lirai, etc.; *Cond.* lirais, etc.
2. *Pres. part.* **lisant;** *Imp. ind.* lisais, etc.; *Pres. subj.* lise, lises, lise, lisions, lisiez, lisent.
3. *Past part.* **lu;** *Past indef.* ai lu, etc.
4. *Pres. ind.* **lis,** lis, lit, lisons, lisez, lisent; *Impv.* lis, lisons, lisez.
5. *Past def.* **lus,** lus, lut, lûmes, lûtes, lurent; *Imp. subj.* lusse, lusses, lût, etc.
Like **lire:** élire, *to elect;* relire, *to reread;* réélire, *to re-elect.*

**24. Mettre,** *to place, to put.*

1. *Inf.* **mettre;** *Fut.* mettrai, etc.; *Cond.* mettrais, etc.

2. *Pres. part.* **mettant;** *Imp. ind.* mettais, etc.; *Pres. subj.* mette, mettes, mette, mettions, mettiez, mettent.

3. *Past part.* **mis;** *Past indef.* ai mis, etc.

4. *Pres. ind.* **mets,** mets, met, mettons, mettez, mettent; *Impv.* mets, mettons, mettez.

5. *Past def.* **mis,** mis, mit, mîmes, mîtes, mirent; *Imp. subj.* misse, misses, mît, etc.

Like **mettre:** admettre, *to admit;* commettre, *to commit;* omettre, *to omit;* permettre, *to permit;* promettre, *to promise;* remettre, *to put back, to hand to;* soumettre, *to submit.*

**25. Mourir,** *to die.*

1. *Inf.* **mourir;** *Fut.* mourrai, etc.; *Cond.* mourrais, etc.

2. *Pres. part.* **mourant;** *Imp. ind.* mourais, etc.; *Pres. subj.* meure, meures, meure, mourions, mouriez, meurent.

3. *Past part.* **mort;** *Past indef.* suis mort, etc.

4. *Pres. ind.* **meurs,** meurs, meurt, mourons, mourez, meurent; *Impv.* meurs, mourons, mourez.

5. *Past def.* **mourus,** mourus, mourut, mourûmes, mourûtes, moururent; *Imp. subj.* mourusse, mourusses, mourût, etc.

Hi Karina

**26. Naître,** *to be born.*

1. *Inf.* **naître;** *Fut.* naîtrai, etc.; *Cond.* naîtrais, etc.

2. *Pres. part.* **naissant;** *Imp. ind.* naissais, etc.; *Pres. subj.* naisse, naisses, naisse, naissions, naissiez, naissent.

3. *Past part.* **né;** *Past indef.* suis né, etc.

4. *Pres. ind.* **nais,** nais, naît, naissons, naissez, naissent; *Impv.* nais, naissons, naissez.

5. *Past def.* **naquis,** naquis, naquit, naquîmes, naquîtes, naquirent; *Imp. subj.* naquisse, naquisses, naquît, etc.

**27. Ouvrir,** *to open.*

1. *Inf.* **ouvrir;** *Fut.* ouvrirai, etc.; *Cond.* ouvrirais, etc.

2. *Pres. part.* **ouvrant;** *Imp. ind.* ouvrais, etc.; *Pres. subj.* ouvre, ouvres, ouvre, ouvrions, ouvriez, ouvrent.

3. *Past part.* **ouvert;** *Past indef.* ai ouvert, etc.

4. *Pres. ind.* **ouvre,** ouvres, ouvre, ouvrons, ouvrez, ouvrent; *Impv.* ouvre, ouvrons, ouvrez.

5. *Past def.* **ouvris,** ouvris, ouvrit, ouvrîmes, ouvrîtes, ouvrirent; *Imp. subj.* ouvrisse, ouvrisses, ouvrît, etc.

Like **ouvrir:** couvrir, *to cover;* découvrir, *to discover, to find out;* offrir, *to offer;* recouvrir, *to cover;* souffrir, *to suffer, to endure.*

**28. Plaire,** *to please.*

1. *Inf.* **plaire;** *Fut.* plairai, etc.; *Cond.* plairais, etc.

2. *Pres. part.* **plaisant;** *Imp. ind.* plaisais, etc.; *Pres. subj.* plaise, plaises, plaise, plaisions, plaisiez, plaisent.

3. *Past part.* **plu;** *Past indef.* ai plu, etc.

4. *Pres. ind.* **plais,** plais, plaît, plaisons, plaisez, plaisent; *Impv.* plais, plaisons, plaisez.

5. *Past def.* **plus,** plus, plut, plûmes, plûtes, plurent; *Imp. subj.* plusse, plusses, plût, etc.

Like **plaire:** déplaire, *to displease;* se taire,[1] *to be silent.*

[1] (Il se) **tait** has no circumflex.

**29. Pleuvoir,** *to rain.*

1. *Inf.* **pleuvoir;** *Fut.* il pleuvra; *Cond.* il pleuvrait.

2. *Pres. part.* **pleuvant;** *Imp. ind.* il pleuvait; *Pres. subj.* il pleuve.

3. *Past part.* **plu;** *Past indef.* il a plu.

4. *Pres. ind.* il **pleut.**

5. *Past def.* il **plut;** *Imp. subj.* il plût.

**30. Pouvoir,** *to be able.*

1. *Inf.* **pouvoir;** *Fut.* pourrai, etc.; *Cond.* pourrais, etc.

2. *Pres. part.* **pouvant;** *Imp. ind.* pouvais, etc.; *Pres. subj.* puisse, puisses, puisse, puissions, puissiez, puissent.

3. *Past part.* **pu;** *Past indef.* ai pu, etc.

4. *Pres. ind.* **puis** *or* **peux,** peux, peut, pouvons, pouvez, peuvent.

5. *Past def.* **pus,** pus, put, pûmes, pûtes, purent; *Imp. subj.* pusse, pusses, pût, etc.

**31. Prendre,** *to take.*

1. *Inf.* **prendre;** *Fut.* prendrai, etc.; *Cond.* prendrais, etc.

2. *Pres. part.* **prenant;** *Imp. ind.* prenais, etc.; *Pres. subj.* prenne, prennes, prenne, prenions, preniez, prennent.

3. *Past part.* **pris;** *Past indef.* ai pris, etc.

4. *Pres. ind.* **prends,** prends, prend, prenons, prenez, prennent; *Impv.* prends, prenons, prenez.

5. *Past def.* **pris,** pris, prit, prîmes, prîtes, prirent; *Imp. subj.* prisse, prisses, prît, etc.

Like **prendre:** apprendre, *to learn;* comprendre, *to understand;* entreprendre, *to undertake;* reprendre, *to take back, to resume;* surprendre, *to surprise.*

**32. Recevoir,** *to receive.*

1. *Inf.* **recevoir;** *Fut.* recevrai, etc.; *Cond.* recevrais, etc.

2. *Pres. part.* **recevant;** *Imp. ind.* recevais, etc.; *Pres. subj.* reçoive, reçoives, reçoive, recevions, receviez, reçoivent.

3. *Past part.* **reçu;** *Past indef.* ai reçu, etc.

4. *Pres. ind.* **reçois,** reçois, reçoit, recevons, recevez, reçoivent; *Impv.* reçois, recevons, recevez.

5. *Past def.* **reçus,** reçus, reçut, reçûmes, reçûtes, reçurent; *Imp. subj.* reçusse, reçusses, reçût, etc.

Like **recevoir:** apercevoir, *to perceive;* concevoir, *to conceive;* décevoir, *to deceive.*

**33. Résoudre,** *to resolve, to solve.*

1. *Inf.* **résoudre;** *Fut.* résoudrai, etc.; *Cond.* résoudrais, etc.
2. *Pres. part.* **résolvant;** *Imp. ind.* résolvais, etc.; *Pres. subj.* résolve, résolves, résolve, résolvions, résolviez, résolvent.
3. *Past part.* **résolu;** *Past indef.* ai résolu, etc.
4. *Pres. ind.* **résous,** résous, résout, résolvons, résolvez, résolvent; *Impv.* résous, résolvons, résolvez.
5. *Past def.* **résolus,** résolus, résolut, résolûmes, résolûtes, résolurent; *Imp. subj.* résolusse, résolusses, résolût, etc.

**34. Rire,** *to laugh.*

1. *Inf.* **rire;** *Fut.* rirai, etc.; *Cond.* rirais, etc.
2. *Pres. part.* **riant;** *Imp. ind.* riais, etc.; *Pres. subj.* rie, ries, rie, riions, riiez, rient.
3. *Past part.* **ri;** *Past indef.* ai ri, etc.
4. *Pres. ind.* **ris,** ris, rit, rions, riez, rient; *Impv.* ris, rions, riez.
5. *Past def.* **ris,** ris, rit, rîmes, rîtes, rirent; *Imp. subj.* risse, risses, rît, etc.

Like **rire:** sourire, *to smile.*

**35. Savoir,** *to know.*

1. *Inf.* **savoir;** *Fut.* saurai, etc.; *Cond.* saurais, etc.
2. *Pres. part.* **sachant;** *Imp. ind.* savais, etc.; *Pres. subj.* sache, saches, sache, sachions, sachiez, sachent.
3. *Past part.* **su;** *Past indef.* ai su, etc.
4. *Pres. ind.* **sais,** sais, sait, savons, savez, savent; *Impv.* sache, sachons, sachez.
5. *Past def.* **sus,** sus, sut, sûmes, sûtes, surent; *Imp. subj.* susse, susses, sût, etc.

**36. Suffire,** *to be sufficient.*

1. *Inf.* **suffire;** *Fut.* suffirai, etc.; *Cond.* suffirais, etc.
2. *Pres. part.* **suffisant;** *Imp. ind.* suffisais, etc.; *Pres. subj.* suffise, suffises, suffise, suffisions, suffisiez, suffisent.
3. *Past part.* **suffi;** *Past indef.* ai suffi, etc.
4. *Pres. ind.* **suffis,** suffis, suffit, suffisons, suffisez, suffisent; *Impv.* suffis, suffisons, suffisez.
5. *Past def.* **suffis,** suffis, suffit, suffîmes, suffîtes, suffirent; *Imp. subj.* suffisse, suffisses, suffît, etc.

**37. Suivre,** *to follow.*

1. *Inf.* **suivre;** *Fut.* suivrai, etc.; *Cond.* suivrais, etc.

2. *Pres. part.* **suivant;** *Imp. ind.* suivais, etc.; *Pres. subj.* suive, suives, suive, suivions, suiviez, suivent.

3. *Past part.* **suivi;** *Past indef.* ai suivi, etc.

4. *Pres. ind.* **suis,** suis, suit, suivons, suivez, suivent; *Impv.* suis, suivons, suivez.

5. *Past def.* **suivis,** suivis, suivit, suivîmes, suivîtes, suivirent; *Imp. subj.* suivisse, suivisses, suivît, etc.

Like **suivre:** poursuivre, *to pursue.*

**38. Tenir,** *to hold.*

1. *Inf.* **tenir;** *Fut.* tiendrai, etc.; *Cond.* tiendrais, etc.

2. *Pres. part.* **tenant;** *Imp. ind.* tenais, etc.; *Pres. subj.* tienne, tiennes, tienne, tenions, teniez, tiennent.

3. *Past part.* **tenu;** *Past indef.* ai tenu, etc.

4. *Pres. ind.* **tiens,** tiens, tient, tenons, tenez, tiennent; *Impv.* tiens, tenons, tenez.

5. *Past def.* **tins,** tins, tint, tînmes, tîntes, tinrent; *Imp. subj.* tinsse, tinsses, tînt, etc.

Like **tenir:** appartenir (à), *to belong (to);* contenir, *to contain;* maintenir, *to maintain;* retenir, *to delay;* obtenir, *to obtain;* soutenir, *to uphold.*

**39. Vaincre,** *to conquer.*

1. *Inf.* **vaincre;** *Fut.* vaincrai, etc.; *Cond.* vaincrais, etc.

2. *Pres. part.* **vainquant;** *Imp. ind.* vainquais, etc.; *Pres. subj.* vainque, vainques, vainque, vainquions, vainquiez, vainquent.

3. *Past part.* **vaincu;** *Past indef.* ai vaincu, etc.

4. *Pres. ind.* **vaincs,** vaincs, vainc, vainquons, vainquez, vainquent; *Impv.* vaincs, vainquons, vainquez.

5. *Past def.* **vainquis,** vainquis, vainquit, vainquîmes, vainquîtes, vainquirent; *Imp. subj.* vainquisse, vainquisses, vainquît, etc.

Like **vaincre:** convaincre, *to convince.*

**40. Valoir,** *to be worth.*

1. *Inf.* **valoir;** *Fut.* vaudrai, etc.; *Cond.* vaudrais, etc.

2. *Pres. part.* **valant;** *Imp. ind.* valais, etc.; *Pres. subj.* vaille, vailles, vaille, valions, valiez, vaillent.

3. *Past part.* **valu;** *Past indef.* ai valu, etc.

4. *Pres. ind.* **vaux,** vaux, vaut, valons, valez, valent; *Impv.* vaux, valons, valez.

5. *Past def.* **valus,** valus, valut, valûmes, valûtes, valurent; *Imp. subj.* valusse, valusses, valût, etc.

Like **valoir:** équivaloir, *to be equivalent to.*

**41. Venir,** *to come.*

1. *Inf.* **venir;** *Fut.* viendrai, etc.; *Cond.* viendrais, etc.

2. *Pres. part.* **venant;** *Imp. ind.* venais, etc.; *Pres. subj.* vienne, viennes, vienne, venions, veniez, viennent.

3. *Past part.* **venu;** *Past indef.* suis venu, etc.

4. *Pres. ind.* **viens,** viens, vient, venons, venez, viennent; *Impv.* viens, venons, venez.

5. *Past def.* **vins,** vins, vint, vînmes, vîntes, vinrent; *Imp. subj.* vinsse, vinsses, vînt, etc.

Like **venir:** convenir, *to be acceptable, agreeable to;* devenir, *to become;* parvenir à, *to succeed in;* prévenir, *to notify, to warn;* provenir, *to come (from), to originate (from);* revenir, *to come back;* se souvenir, *to remember.*

**42. Vêtir,** *to clothe.*

1. *Inf.* **vêtir;** *Fut.* vêtirai, etc.; *Cond.* vêtirais, etc.

2. *Pres. part.* **vêtant;** *Imp. ind.* vêtais, etc.; *Pres. subj.* vête, vêtes, vête, vêtions, vêtiez, vêtent.

3. *Past part.* **vêtu;** *Past indef.* ai vêtu, etc.

4. *Pres. ind.* **vêts,** vêts, vêt, vêtons, vêtez, vêtent; *Impv.* vêts, vêtons, vêtez.

5. *Past def.* **vêtis,** vêtis, vêtit, vêtîmes, vêtîtes, vêtirent; *Imp. subj.* vêtisse, vêtisses, vêtît, etc.

Like **vêtir:** revêtir, *to put on.*

**43. Vivre,** *to live.*

1. *Inf.* **vivre;** *Fut.* vivrai, etc.; *Cond.* vivrais, etc.

2. *Pres. part.* **vivant;** *Imp. ind.* vivais, etc.; *Pres. subj.* vive, vives, vive, vivions, viviez, vivent.

3. *Past part.* **vécu;** *Past indef.* ai vécu, etc.

4. *Pres. ind.* **vis,** vis, vit, vivons, vivez, vivent; *Impv.* vis, vivons, vivez.

5. *Past def.* **vécus,** vécus, vécut, vécûmes, vécûtes, vécurent; *Imp. subj.* vécusse, vécusses, vécût, etc.

Like **vivre:** survivre, *to survive.*

**44. Voir,** *to see.*

1. *Inf.* **voir;** *Fut.* verrai, etc.; *Cond.* verrais, etc.

2. *Pres. part.* **voyant;** *Imp. ind.* voyais, etc.; *Pres. subj.* voie, voies, voie, voyions, voyiez, voient.

3. *Past part.* **vu;** *Past indef.* ai vu, etc.

4. *Pres. ind.* **vois,** vois, voit, voyons, voyez, voient; *Impv.* vois, voyons, voyez.

5. *Past def.* **vis,** vis, vit, vîmes, vîtes, virent; *Imp. subj.* visse, visses, vît, etc.

Like **voir:** revoir, *to see again.*

**45. Vouloir,** *to want.*

1. *Inf.* **vouloir;** *Fut.* voudrai, etc.; *Cond.* voudrais, etc.

# APPENDIX II

2. *Pres. part.* **voulant**; *Imp. ind.* voulais, etc.; *Pres. subj.* veuille, veuilles, veuille, voulions, vouliez, veuillent.

3. *Past part.* **voulu**; *Past indef.* ai voulu, etc.

4. *Pres. ind.* **veux**, veux, veut, voulons, voulez, veulent; *Impv.* veuillez, *have the kindness to, be good enough to.*

5. *Past def.* **voulus**, voulus, voulut, voulûmes, voulûtes, voulurent; *Imp. subj.* voulusse, voulusses, voulût, etc.


## INDEX OF IRREGULAR VERBS

### (Figures refer to paragraphs in this appendix.)

# APPENDIX III

## THE GOVERNMENT OF FOLLOWING INFINITIVES

*A.* Reference list of verbs governing a following infinitive without any preposition:

| | | |
|---|---|---|
| accourir | entendre | reconnaître |
| affirmer | envoyer | regarder |
| aimer | espérer | rentrer |
| aimer autant | faillir | retourner |
| aimer mieux | faire | revenir |
| aller | falloir | savoir |
| apercevoir | figurer (se) | sembler |
| assurer | imaginer (s') | sentir |
| avoir beau | juger | souhaiter |
| avouer | justifier | soutenir |
| censé: être — | laisser | supposé: être — |
| compter | mener | supposer |
| confesser | monter | témoigner |
| courir | nier | trouver (se) |
| croire | oser | valoir autant |
| daigner | paraître | valoir mieux |
| déclarer | penser | venir |
| descendre | pouvoir | voir |
| désirer | préférer | voler |
| devoir | prétendre | vouloir |
| écouter | rappeler (se) | |

*B.* Reference list of verbs governing a following infinitive by *à:*

| | | |
|---|---|---|
| abaisser (s') | aimer | aspirer |
| abandonner (s') | amener | attacher (s') |
| aboutir | amuser (s') | attendre (s') |
| abuser (s') | appeler | autoriser |
| accord: être d'— | appliquer (s') | avoir |
| accorder (s') | apprendre | balancer |
| accoutumer (s') | apprêter (s') | borner (se) |
| aider | arrêter (s') | chercher |

148

commencer
*condamner
conduire
*consacrer
consentir
consister
conspirer
continuer
contraindre
contribuer
*décider
demeurer
dépenser
destiner
*déterminer
dévouer (se)
différer
*disposer
divertir (se)
donner
*employer
encourager
*engager
enseigner
*entraîner
être
exceller
*exciter
*exercer

exhorter
*exposer
fatiguer (se)
forcer
gagner
*habituer
haïr
hésiter
inciter
incliner
instruire
*intéresser
inviter
jouer
*mettre
montrer
*obliger
obstiner (s')
*occuper
offrir (s')
parvenir
*passer
peine: avoir (de la) —
pencher
penser
perdre
persévérer
persister

plaire (se)
plier (se)
porter
pousser
prendre plaisir
prendre (se)
*préparer
procéder
provoquer
recommencer
réduire
*refuser
renoncer
résigner (se)
*résoudre
rester
réussir
risquer (se)
servir
songer
suffire
surprendre
tarder
tendre
tenir
travailler
*trouver
venir
viser

## C. Reference list of verbs governing a following infinitive by *de:*

accorder
*accuser
achever
affecter
affliger (s')
*applaudir
*arrêter
*attrister

avertir
blâmer
brûler
censurer
cesser
*charger
choisir
commander

conseiller
consoler
contenter (se)
convaincre
convenir
craindre
crier
décider

* The asterisk indicates that the verb may also be used reflexively with this preposition.

*décourager
dédaigner
*défendre
*défier
dégoûter
délibérer
demander
dépêcher (se)
désespérer
déterminer
détester
détourner
dire
dispenser
dissuader
douter (se)
écrire
efforcer (s')
effrayer (s')
*empêcher
empresser (s')
ennuyer (s')
entreprendre
essayer
étonner (s')
éviter
*excuser
exempter
faire bien
fatiguer (se)
feindre
finir
forcer
frémir
garder (se)

gronder
hâter (se)
impatienter (s')
indigner (s')
inspirer
interdire
jouir
juger bon
jurer
lasser (se)
louer
manquer
méditer
mêler (se)
menacer
mériter
*moquer
mourir
négliger
obtenir
occuper (s')
offrir
omettre
ordonner
oublier
pardonner
parier
parler
passer (se)
*permettre
persuader
piquer (se)
*plaindre
prendre garde
prendre soin

prescrire
*presser
présumer
prier
priver (se)
projeter
*promettre
*proposer
protester
punir
recommander
refuser
regretter
réjouir (se)
remercier
repentir (se)
reprendre
réprimander
*reprocher
résoudre
rire
risquer
rougir
soucier (se)
souffrir
soupçonner
sourire
souvenir (se)
suggérer
supplier
tâcher
tenter
trembler
trouver bon
venir

# APPENDIX IV

## THE GOVERNMENT OF VERBAL OBJECTS

**How to Use This Table:**

The student has already encountered examples of the differences between English and French in the way that verbs govern their objects. English says, *to look for something;* French says **chercher quelque chose.** On the other hand English says, *to obey someone;* French says, **obéir à quelqu'un.** Some of the most important verbs showing such differences have been listed in the following table. It is suggested that the student learn the whole formula, e.g., **demander à quelqu'un de faire quelque chose,** especially when the government of a following infinitive is also involved. **Quelque chose** (abbreviated to **qqch**) always represents an object that is a *thing;* **quelqu'un** (abbreviated to **qqn**) always represents an object that is a *person.* This list is not intended to be complete; the student will come across and learn other verbs showing comparable differences in the course of his reading.

**acheter**
qqch à qqn               *to buy something for (from) someone*

**agir (s') (impersonal)**
de qqn (qqch)         *to be a question of someone (something)*

**aider**
qqn                     *to help someone*
(à) qqn à faire qqch     *to help someone to do something*

**apercevoir (s')**
de qqch              *to perceive (become aware of) something*

**appartenir**
à qqn                  *to belong to someone*

**apprendre**
qqch à qqn           *to teach someone something*
qqch de qqn          *to learn something from someone*
à qqn à faire qqch     *to teach someone to do something*

**approcher (s')**
de qqn (qqch)         *to approach someone (something)*

**assister**
 à qqch — *to be present at something*
**attendre**
 qqn (qqch) — *to wait for someone (something)*
**attendre (s')**
 à (faire) qqch — *to expect (to do) something*
**avoir besoin**
 de qqn (qqch) — *to need someone (something)*
**avoir envie**
 de faire qqch — *to have a desire to do something*
**avoir honte**
 de qqn (qqch) — *to be ashamed of someone (something)*
**avoir peur**
 de qqn (qqch) — *to be afraid of someone (something)*
**cacher**
 qqch à qqn — *to hide something from someone*
**chercher**
 qqn (qqch) — *to look for someone (something)*
**commander**
 à qqn de faire qqch — *to command someone to do something*
**conseiller**
 à qqn de faire qqch — *to advise someone to do something*
**craindre**
 qqn (qqch) — *to be afraid of someone (something)*
**défendre**
 à qqn de faire qqch — *to forbid someone to do something*
**demander**
 qqch à qqn — *to ask someone for something*
 à qqn de faire qqch — *to ask someone to do something*
 à faire qqch — *to ask to do something*
**dépendre**
 de qqn (qqch) — *to depend on someone (something)*
**descendre** — *to go down* (intransitive; aux. **être**)
 qqch (aux. **avoir**) — *to bring (take) something down*
**devoir**
 qqch à qqn — *to owe someone something*
**dévouer (se)**
 à qqn (qqch) — *to devote oneself to someone (something)*
**dire**
 qqch à qqn — *to say something to someone* / *to tell something to someone*

| | |
|---|---|
| qqch de qqn | *to say something about someone* |
| à qqn de faire qqch | *to tell someone to do something* |
| **donner** | |
| qqch à qqn | *to give someone something* |
| **douter** | |
| de qqch | *to doubt something* |
| **douter (se)** | |
| de qqch | *to suspect something* |
| **échapper** | |
| à qqn | *to escape (from) someone* |
| **écouter** | |
| qqn (qqch) | *to listen to someone (something)* |
| **écrire** | |
| qqch à qqn | *to write something to someone* |
| au sujet de qqn (qqch) | *to write about someone (something)* |
| à qqn de faire qqch | *to write someone to do something* |
| **empêcher** | |
| qqn de faire qqch | *to prevent someone from doing something* |
| **enseigner** | |
| qqn | *to teach someone* |
| qqch à qqn | *to teach someone something* |
| à qqn à faire qqch | *to teach someone to do something* |
| **essayer** | |
| qqch | *to try something on (out)* |
| de faire qqch | *to try to do something* |
| **faire attention** | |
| à qqn (qqch) | *to pay attention to someone (something)* |
| **faire plaisir** | |
| à qqn | *to please someone* |
| **faire (se)** | |
| à qqch | *to get used to something* |
| **falloir (impersonal)** | |
| qqch | *something to be needed, to be necessary* |
| qqch à qqn | *something to be needed by (necessary for) someone* |
| **insister** | |
| sur qqch | *to insist on something* |
| **intéresser (s')** | |
| à qqn (qqch) | *to be interested in someone (something)* |
| **inviter** | |
| qqn à faire qqch | *to invite someone to do something* |

**jouer**
  à qqch                      *to play (a game)*
  de qqch                   *to play (an instrument)*

**jouir**
  de qqch                   *to enjoy something*

**laisser**
  qqn (qqch)               *to leave someone (something)*
  qqn faire qqch          *to let someone do something*

**lire**
  qqch à qqn              *to read something to someone*
  qqch sur qqch         *to read something about something*

**manquer**
  de qqch                   *to lack something*

**médire**
  de qqn                    *to slander someone*

**mentir**
  à qqn                     *to lie to someone*
  à qqn au sujet de qqch  *to lie to someone about something*

**mettre**
  qqn (au courant de qqch)  *to inform someone (about something)*
  qqch                       { *to put or place something*
                            { *to put on something*

**monter**                 *to go up* (intransitive; aux. **être**)
  qqch (aux. **avoir**)      *to bring (take) something up*

**montrer**
  qqch à qqn             { *to show something to someone*
                          { *to show someone something*

**obéir**
  à qqn (qqch)            *to obey someone (something)*

**obtenir**
  qqch pour qqn         *to get something for someone*
  qqch de qqn           *to get something from someone*

**occuper (s')**
  de qqn (qqch)          *to take care of someone (something)*

**offrir**
  qqch à qqn              *to offer someone something*
  à qqn de faire qqch    *to offer to do something for someone*

**ordonner**
  à qqn de faire qqch    *to order someone to do something*

**ouvrir**
  qqch à qqn              *to open something to someone*

**parler**
  qqch (a language)                   *to speak something*
  à qqn                             *to speak to someone*
  de qqn (qqch)                 *to speak of someone (something)*

**passer** (se)
  de qqn (qqch)                 *to do without someone (something)*

**payer**
  qqch                            *to pay for something*
  qqch à qqn                    *to pay someone for something*
  qqn (if the thing paid for     *to pay someone*
    is not mentioned)

**penser**
  à qqn (qqch)                  *to think of someone (something)*
                               *(have in mind)*
  de qqn (qqch)                 *to think of someone (something)*
                               *(have an opinion)*

**permettre**
  à qqn de faire qqch          *to permit someone to do something*

**plaindre** (se)
  de qqn (qqch)                 *to complain of someone (something)*

**plaire**
  à qqn                               *to please someone*

**prendre**
  qqch à qqn                    *to take something from someone*

**présenter**
  qqn à qqn                     *to present (introduce) someone to someone*
  qqch à qqn                    *to present someone with something*

**prier**
  qqn de faire qqch            *to ask someone to do something*

**promettre**
  qqch à qqn                    *to promise someone something*
  à qqn de faire qqch          *to promise someone to do something*

**punir**
  qqn de qqch                   *to punish someone for something*

**rappeler** (se)
  qqn (qqch)                    *to remember someone (something)*

**refuser**
  qqch à qqn                    *to refuse someone something*
  de faire qqch                 *to refuse to do something*
  à qqn de faire qqch          *to refuse someone to do something*

**regarder**
  qqn (qqch)                    *to look at someone (something)*

**regretter**
  qqch — *to regret something*
  qqn — *to miss someone*
**remercier**
  qqn de qqch — *to thank someone for something*
**rentrer** — *to go back (home); to go in again* (intransitive; aux. **être**)
  qqch — *to take something in* (transitive; aux. **avoir**)

**répondre**
  qqch — *to answer something* (the exact words are quoted)
  à qqch — *to answer something* (e.g., a question)
  à qqn — *to answer someone*
  qqch à qqn — *to answer something to someone*
**ressembler**
  à qqn (qqch) — *to resemble someone (something)*
**satisfaire**
  qqch — *to satisfy something* (e.g., one's curiosity)
  qqn — *to satisfy someone* (e.g., one's professor)
  à qqch — *to do one's duty to something* (e.g., one's conscience)

**savoir**
  qqch — *to know something*
  faire qqch — *to know how to do something*
**savoir gré**
  à qqn de qqch — *to be grateful to someone for something*
**servir (se)**
  de qqn (qqch) — *to use someone (something)*
**songer**
  à qqn (qqch) — *to think (dream) of someone (something)*
  à faire qqch — *to think of doing something*
**sortir** — *to go out* (intransitive; aux. **être**)
  qqch — *to take out something* (transitive; aux. **avoir**)

**souhaiter**
  qqch à qqn — *to wish someone something*
**souvenir (se)**
  de qqn (qqch) — *to remember someone (something)*
**survivre**
  à qqn (qqch) — *to survive someone (something)*

**téléphoner**
  à qqn                   *to telephone (to) someone*
**tenir**
  à qqn                   *to be fond of someone*
  à qqch                 *to want (like) something*
  à faire qqch           *to be anxious to do something*
**vendre**
  qqch à qqn             *to sell something to someone*

# APPENDIX V

## THE GOVERNMENT OF PREPOSITIONAL COMPLE-MENTS OF ADJECTIVES

An adjective is often followed by a complement that is connected to it by a preposition. Although general rules may be laid down to help the student to decide which preposition to use, it is probably best to remember individual cases as they arise. In a short time the student should not hesitate over the preposition to use with the most common adjectives.

### A. Adjective + *à* + complement.

When the adjective expresses fitness, tendency (or their opposites), comparison, etc., it is likely to govern its complement by à.

| | |
|---|---|
| Il est *inférieur aux* autres. | *He is inferior to the others.* |
| Il est *bon à* quelque chose. | *He is good for something.* |
| Les livres sont *utiles aux* étudiants. | *Books are useful to students.* |

accoutumé, *accustomed (to)*
agréable, *pleasant (to)*
bon, *good, fit (for)*
convenable, *suitable (to)*
égal, *equal (to)*
favorable, *favorable (to)*
fidèle, *faithful (in)*

habile, *clever (in)*
impropre, *unfit (for)*
inférieur, *inferior (to)*
infidèle, *unfaithful (to)*
inutile, *useless (to)*
lent, *slow (in)*
pareil, *similar (to)*

prêt, *ready (to)*
prompt, *prompt (in)*
propre, *fit (for)*
semblable, *similar (to)*
supérieur, *superior (to)*
utile, *useful (to)*
etc.

### B. Adjective + *de* + complement.

When the adjective expresses source, origin, sentiment, abundance, separation, distance, want, etc., it is likely to govern its complement by de.

| | |
|---|---|
| Je suis *content de* cette lettre. | *I am pleased with this letter.* |
| Il est *absent de* la ville. | *He is absent from the city.* |
| Il est *indigne de* toute récompense. | *He is unworthy of all reward.* |

158

# APPENDIX V

absent, *absent (from)*
affligé, *grieved (at)*
capable, *capable (of)*
charmé, *delighted (with)*
confus, *confused (at)*
content, *pleased (at)*
contrarié, *vexed (with)*
dépourvu, *devoid (of)*
désireux, *desirous (of)*
différent, *different (from)*
digne, *worthy (of)*
éloigné, *distant (from)*
enchanté, *delighted (with)*
ennuyé, *weary (of)*
étonné, *astonished (at)*
exempt, *free (from)*
fâché, *sorry (for)*

fier, *proud (of)*
heureux, *glad (of)*
honteux, *ashamed (of)*
ignorant, *ignorant (of)*
inconnu, *unknown (to)*
indigne, *unworthy (of)*
inquiet, *uneasy (about)*
jaloux, *jealous (of)*
libre, *free (from)*
offensé, *offended (at)*
plein, *full (of)*
ravi, *delighted (with)*
satisfait, *satisfied (with)*
sûr, *sure (of)*
surpris, *surprised (at)*
triste, *sad (at)*
vide, *empty (of)*
etc.

## C. Other Prepositions.

1) *Fâché contre* quelqu'un.     *Angry with (at) someone.*
2) *Bon pour* quelqu'un.     *Kind to (good for) someone.*
3) **Envers** governs the complements of adjectives expressing disposition or feeling towards someone or something.

Il est *juste envers* tous.     *He is just to all.*

bon, *kind*
charitable, *charitable*
cruel, *cruel*
dur, *hard, harsh*
généreux, *generous*
indulgent, *indulgent*
insolent, *insolent*

juste, *just*
libéral, *liberal*
méchant, *malicious*
poli, *polite*
reconnaissant, *grateful*
respectueux, *respectful*
sévère, *severe, stern*
etc.

# INDEX

Numbers refer to sections in the grammar.

161

# INDEX

Dimension, methods of indicating, **57**
**dont, 41***C*

Ellipsis, defined, Intr. **X**
**en,** as preposition with geographical names, **4**; as substitute for partitive noun, **9**; adverbial use, **34***A*; used as pronoun, **34***C*; agreement of past participle after **en, 85***B*; as preposition followed by present participle, **115**
**être,** conjugation, App. **I***B*; as auxiliary verb, **83***B*; agreement of past participle in verbs conjugated with **être, 85**
Expressions of quantity, **10**

**faire,** use with dependent infinitive, **113**
**falloir,** uses, **106**; contrasted with **devoir, 108**
Fractions, **45**
Future, forms, **62**; uses, **63, 64**; in conditional sentences, **65**; implied future, **68**; expressing possibility, **69**

**il y a,** use, **105***B*
Imperative, **61**
Imperfect indicative, forms, **74***A*; use in conditional sentences, **76***A*; use with **depuis,** etc., **76***B*; use in indirect discourse, **76***C*; other uses, **76***D, E, F, G*; contrasted with past indefinite, **77**
Impersonal verb, forms and uses, **105**; governing subjunctive of personal feeling, **97**; governing subjunctive of possibility, **99**
Indefinite pronoun, defined, Intr. **III** *G*; **même, 81**; **tel, 82**; **autre, 87**; **quelqu'un (quelque), 88**; followed by **de** + adjective, **89**; **chacun (chaque), 90**; **n'importe qui (lequel, quoi, quel), 114**; **tout, 124**
Indicative mood, definition, **58**; replacing subjunctive, **92***B*

Infinitive, replacing subjunctive, **92***A, C, D*; use after **laisser,** etc., **112**; use after **faire, 113**; use after prepositions, **116**; dependent upon a verb, **117**; dependent upon a noun or adjective, **118**
Interjection, defined, Intr. **IX**
Interrogative adjective, **quel,** etc., **54**
Interrogative pronoun, defined, Intr. **III***B*; **qui** and **que,** as relative and interrogative pronoun, contrasted, **49**; construction and use of reduplicated forms, **50**; object of preposition, **51**; translation of *whose ?*, **51***B*; definitions, **52**; indirect questions, **53**; **lequel ?, 54**
Interrogative word order, **55**

**laisser,** uses, **112**
**le,** use as pronoun, **33**
**lequel,** etc., relative pronoun, **41***E*; interrogative pronoun, **54**

**même,** uses, **81**
Mood (mode), of verbs, defined, Intr. **V**

Names, proper, plural, **26***D*
**ne,** used alone, **14**; pleonastic, **15, 28***A* 3, **94**
Negatives, forms, **11**; position, **12**; **ne** used alone, **14**; pleonastic **ne, 15, 28***A* 3, **94**
**n'importe qui (lequel, quoi, quel), 114**
Noun, defined, Intr. **II**; gender, **24**; formation of feminine, **25**; formation of plural, **26**; governing dependent infinitive, **118**
Numerals, cardinal, **43**; ordinals, **44**; fractions, **45**; arithmetic, **46**

**on,** replacing passive, **86***E* 1
**où, 41***D*

**par,** used after **commencer** and **finir, 116***C*

162